The Gideon In You

God can use you for His Glory...

Jason L. Lohorn

Aventine Press

Copyright © 2011 by Jason L. Lohorn

First Edition

Without limiting the rights under copyright reserved above, no part of this publication may be reproduced, stored in or introduced into a retrieval system, or transmitted, in any form or by any means (electronic, mechanical, photocopying, recording, or otherwise), without the prior written permission of both the copyright owner and the publisher of this book.

Published by Aventine Press
750 State Street #319
San Diego CA, 92010
www.aventinepress.com

ISBN: 1-59330-733-0
Printed in the United States of America

ALL RIGHTS RESERVED

Acknowledgments

During my lifetime I have been blessed to be influenced by so many great people and congregations. These same people have invested in me, prayed for me and given me opportunities to serve the Lord in their presence, churches from Middle Tennessee like Indian Creek Baptist Church, Calvary Baptist Church, Rocky Valley Baptist Church, Upper Helton Baptist Church and my present congregation First Baptist Church Gordonsville. These loving people have allowed me to serve them on the Lord's behalf and I am grateful.

Many pastors have also blessed me over the years. The one pastor that I will mention is Bro. Oscar Trainer, the man of God that led me to the Lord. I remember how he cared for the people of Indian Creek Baptist Church. He was truly a pastor and a shepherd to God's people.

I also appreciate the support of a loving family. God knew what He was doing when He gave me such a wonderful wife that provides strength to our home and allows me to serve the Lord unconditionally. My wife, Nikki, also believes in me. She'll never know how much her faith in me encourages me to keep following God. I am also thankful for my three daughters who do a good job of keeping me humble. I appreciate the love they have for me and more importantly, our Lord.

This book is my first and prayerfully will not be my last. I don't pretend to have a long list of credentials that would suggest the content of this book is scholarly or even interesting. What I do offer is a book that was placed upon my heart to be written to people that are called to live for God and not themselves. In the same way the Holy Spirit helps me write sermons and preach messages, He helped me write these words.

I also want to thank Nakia Vensel and Creative Graphics of Lebanon Tennessee for the artwork that you see on the book cover. The image of a broken pitcher on the ground along with a soldier holding a trumpet and a torch really illustrates this book. Thank you Nakia for capturing on print what I saw in my heart.

Last, but certainly not least, I would like to thank the Lord for not only saving me but also for calling me to preach. His faithfulness to me is without spot. His commitment to giving me something to preach in the pulpit week after week staggers my mind. Hundreds of sermons later, He is still faithful. I also want to thank the Lord for His direction in my life. God saw the Gideon in me and called me to live that kind of life, a life that is invested in the Kingdom.

Introduction

If I had one dollar for every person that asked, "Why would God want to use me?" I would be the richest man on the planet. In the fall of 1998 I was asking myself this very question. Over the course of two years God was following me, pursuing me, all along calling me. His desire was to use me for His glory. Can you imagine that, me, for His glory? Why would God want to use me?

Little did I know, God had been preparing me for years to be a leader in His kingdom agenda. His agenda, you ask? Redeeming and reconciling mankind to Himself. Gods' command, win and baptize disciples in His name, not to mention teach them all that He has taught me. With the Lord's command came a deep conviction in my heart. My life needs to change. How am I suppose to teach others when I myself can barely find Matthew, Mark, Luke and John in my newly purchased bible? My prayer, "Lord replace my desires with your desires." He did it! God did the miraculous. He took away my love for University of Kentucky basketball and golf overnight. Suddenly I found myself reading with a pile of books at the kitchen table instead of being glued to the television set. One of God's principles was established forever in my heart, what God calls you to do, He will help you do.

As I began to ponder God's call on my life, I began to seek counsel from those who had traveled this road. Immediately I was drawn to a High School friend who had been living for the Lord and had received a similar call from God. His advice was for me to read Judges Chapter six, the story of Gideon. God had called Gideon to do something great for His people, Gideon felt inadequate, but God helped Gideon become victorious.

When I read the story of Gideon I realized that God could use me, and If God could use me then God could use anyone. This premise was the basis of one of my first sermons. The sermon introduced men of the bible such as Moses, Gideon and Peter who felt as if God had made a mistake in choosing them as leaders. The central text was from 1 Corinthians 1:26-29.

"For you see your calling, brethren, that not many wise according to the flesh, not many mighty, not many noble, are called. But God has chosen the foolish things of the world to put to shame the wise, and God has chosen the weak things of the world to put to shame the things which are mighty; and the base things of the world and the things which are despised God has chosen, and the things which are not, to bring to nothing the things that are, that no flesh should glory in His presence." 1 Cor. 1:26-29 ,NKJV

As I studied Gideon's' life I began to see some parallels. Gideon like me needed increased faith. So I, like Gideon asked God for signs to confirm His call upon my life. Don't ask me why, but God obliged me in my requests. Through various signs and wonders God not only confirmed His call upon my life, He enthusiastically placed an exclamation point at the end of each encounter. God did the same for Gideon and from

1999 on; I began to see the Gideon in me. A person that was weak in the flesh but growing stronger in the Lord.

Let's fast forward to the year 2003. My wife Nikki and I are now expecting our third child. Our first two children were girls, so now we find ourselves thinking about a boy. Would God give us a boy or girl? If a boy, what would we name him? My vote was for Gideon. I know, you don't like the name. Not only did my wife not like the name, our church wasn't excited about it either. During the fall of 2003 I was preaching a revival at a sister church, guess what? They didn't like the name. I was in the minority. I was not going to have a baby boy named Gideon. In January of 2004 my wife delivered our third child, a baby girl we quickly named Hannah.

Later that same year I was reading my bible through and had come to the book of Judges. As I came to the sixth chapter God began to show me sermons. In fact, the Holy Spirit outlined six sermons within about 45 minutes. The excitement built from one sermon to another, then another. Next thing you know I have a sermon series entitled "The Gideon In You". I started praising God for His precious gift. Then, in my office that day, I heard His voice speak to my heart and say, "write a book about Gideon, here is your baby".

My prayer is that this book, my first project, will be a blessing to you. My desire is that you will discover the potential God sees in your life and realize that there is a Gideon in you. You can be used by God.

Contents

Introduction   V

Part 1 - God Calls Us to Salvation

Chapter 1 :	The Need	3
Chapter 2 :	The Cry	7
Chapter 3 :	The Conviction	11
Chapter 4 :	The Savior Provided	15
Chapter 5 :	The Deliverance Promised	21

Part 2 - God Blesses Those that Give

Chapter 6 :	The Offering Prepared	31
Chapter 7 :	The Miracle Performed	39

Part 3 - God Tests Those He Calls

Chapter 8 :	Why a Test?	47
Chapter 9 :	Gideon's First Assignment - One of Destruction	51
Chapter 10:	Gideon's Second Assignment - One of Construction	55
Chapter 11:	Passing the Test = Blessing	59

Part 4 - God Calls Us to Serve

Chapter 12:	The Goal is Serving not Training	65
Chapter 13:	When You Serve, You Become a Target	69
Chapter 14:	When You Serve, God Shows Up	73
Chapter 15:	Why Do Some Fail to Serve?	77

Part 5 - God Grows Our Faith

Chapter 16:	Victory Without Faith is Impossible	85
Chapter 17:	Asking By Faith - Gideon asks for two signs	89
Chapter 18:	God Will Bless the Right Motive	95

Part 6 - God's Way is the Only Way

Chapter 19:	Reduction Is Necessary for Victory	103
Chapter 20:	God's Keep's His Promises	113
Chapter 21:	Victory - God's Way	119

Section One

"God Calls Us To Salvation"

Chapter One

The Need

Judges 6:1-6a, NKJV

"Then the children of Israel did evil in the sight of the LORD. So the LORD delivered them into the hand of Midian for seven years, and the hand of Midian prevailed against Israel. Because of the Midianites, the children of Israel made for themselves the dens, the caves, and the strongholds, which are in the mountains. So it was, whenever Israel had sown, Midianites would come up; also Amalekites and the people of the East would come up against them. Then they would encamp against them and destroy the produce of the earth as far as Gaza, and leave no sustenance for Israel, neither sheep nor ox nor donkey. For they would come up with their livestock and their tents, coming in as numerous as locusts; both they and their camels were without number; and they would enter the land to destroy it. So Israel was greatly impoverished because of the Midianites, and the children of Israel cried out to the LORD."

Since the beginning of time, man has searched for God, longed for God and truly needed God. Most of the time we discover that we really need God because we have unmet needs. We need something. Usually we discover that we need someone, God. And so, we cry out to God because we have a need, we need help, most of all, we need a savior, someone who can bail us out, someone who can save the day, someone who can right the wrong.

The children of Israel had a great need. In Judges 6:1-6 we see the children of Israel's need. After many years of peace, the children of Israel become complacent, lazy if you will. They begin to turn away from the one true living God and begin to serve false gods. At this point Israel had multiple needs.

The Midianites and the Amalekites were nomad tribes or people groups. They wandered throughout the land devouring every resource in sight. They were consuming other people's food, crops and produce. They would come into the land and take real estate. They would take herds and animals away from their rightful owner. They were absolutely evil. It reminds me of the bully in fifth grade that takes other kids lunch money. You know the type; they take whatever they want because they are bigger and meaner than anybody else, even the teachers sometimes. The Midianites and Amalekites were evil, they were bullies.

Secondly, not only were these nomads evil they were innumerable the Bible says. They were like locusts devouring a crop. There were too many to count and too many to fight. No one could stop them, except God.

The problem is, God in Judges 6:1 delivered the children of Israel into the Midianites hands. Why? Why would God who is loving and holy deliver His own people into the hands of an enemy? The answer, God is a jealous God. Israel had done evil in the sight of the Lord. They had turned away from God and had begun to take part in idol worship. Friend, if you want to make God mad put something or someone before Him. God will not be second in your life, He absolutely will not. The children of Israel had abandoned God and later in Judges 6 God sends them a prophet to give them the bad news.

Meanwhile, this turning away from God has produced a need in the lives of Israel. The need: they needed to be rescued, they need to be delivered, and they needed to be saved from the power of the enemy. The bottom line is this, Israel had a great need. They were overcome by evil and they needed to be saved from it.

Today, many people have a very similar need. People have a need for God to deliver them. Although they may not have tribes of nomads taking their crops, land and animals, they do have an enemy that is trying to take everything they have and everything God desires for them to possess. The enemy is Sin. The Midianites and Amalekites were devastating Israel. Today sin and the bondage of sin, is devastating people all over the world.

Israel's enemy oppressed them, discouraged them and dominated them. Fear was in the hearts of God's people even to the point that they were hiding in caves. There was total intimidation and domination by the enemy. Today, sin and the lifestyle of sin oppresses, discourages and dominates people's lives, leaving them in total despair. As the Midianites stripped the land of its worth, and stripped the people of their possessions, sin strips people today.

Sin destroys relationships.
Sin steals happiness.
Sin oppresses joy.
Sin separates a person from God.
Sin results in death.

When a person walks opposite of God, or chooses to sin or live a life of sin, it opens the door for the enemy. One definition of sin is: thoughts or behavior, which are contrary to the glory or character of God, or to commit an offense against God's laws. The bible, throughout its pages, declares that man is sinful. Romans 14:23b broadens the definition by saying, *"for whatever is not from faith is sin"*.

James 4:17 says, *"Therefore, to him who knows to do good and does not do it, to him it is sin."*

There are consequences to sin. Israel's consequence was the plundering of their possessions by the Midianites and Amalekites. Because God's people turned away from Him, He allowed the enemy to walk right through Israel's front door.

This sin, this oppression by the enemy created a great need for the nation Israel. They needed to be delivered and they needed to be saved. Today, all over the world people need to be saved from sin and it's devastating power. The problem is this; most people aren't so sure they need saving. Many people fail to look inside their heart and see the need to be saved. The need to be delivered by God, the need to be rescued from sin and its eternal death sentence is an incredible need.

If you are a follower of Christ, a Christian, you had this great need in your life before you accepted Jesus Christ as your personal savior. In fact, a person cannot get saved unless they face the music and realize that they are a sinner and have need of a savior. God helps people with this identification of the need by drawing them to Himself by the power of the Holy Spirit. The Holy Spirit of God convicts a person of their sin and reveals this great need for forgiveness, deliverance and salvation.

Israel discovered their great need for God, the need for God's help. It all starts with the need. The need for God to do that which only God can do. It begins with the need.

Chapter Two
The Cry
___

Judges 6:6a, NKJV

"...and the children of Israel cried out to the Lord"

 The Israelites finally had seen enough and suffered enough. Their state was one of humility. They were flat on their backs. Their need was more than they alone could handle. And out of a great need and desperation the people of God finally cry out to the Lord. They cried out to the one they had abandoned. They cried out to the one they had sinned against. The children of Israel needed God's grace and favor upon their lives. In a time of great need their only hope was to cry out to the Lord for deliverance.
 This cry out to the Lord is the God-given route to salvation. Israel's sin and the oppression of that sin had led to horrific consequences. The people were hopeless and in despair. The false gods and idols they had been worshipping were silent.

When all else had failed the people finally turn to God for deliverance.

Doesn't that sound familiar? Do you recognize this path? When a person puts their hope in the things of man or the things of this world, without knowing it they volunteer to take this path. It's a dark and dangerous path. The path of sin leads to difficult consequences and trying circumstances. When a person chooses the path of sin, God chooses to allow those circumstances to flow. The enemy, Satan, authors the evil while God providentially allows the trial to play out. Satan's goal is for the person to keep traveling down the path of sin with no regard to God or repentance. Satan knows that the penalty of sin is death, so he continues his assault. God on the other hand starts drawing the person to the truth. God's desire is for the person to come to the conclusion that they need Him. God is listening for a person's cry for deliverance. God's waiting for the person to get to the end of self. As long as the person thinks they can handle the heat they are on their own.

When I was in the sixth grade I noticed that all of my friends were wearing a popular windbreaker. The jacket had our school name and mascot printed on the front, while a persons last name was written on the back. I had to have one. My nickname growing up was Pee-Wee. Every time I saw one of those jackets I could just picture Pee-Wee written across the back of my jacket. The only problem was the cost of the jacket. I begged my mom for weeks to buy me the jacket. Like most moms, she gave in and made the purchase. Two days later someone steals my coat. Why would someone want to steal a jacket with Pee-Wee written on the back? Who, other than myself, would be proud to wear a jacket with that type of nickname plastered on it? Even more troubling, what would I tell my mom? This jacket was a real sacrifice for her and now

I had worn it for two days and now it's gone. I did what many kids do, I lied. I told my mom that I had forgotten the jacket and left it in my locker. She bought that lie the first day, but knew something was wrong on day two.

She decided to punish me for irresponsibly leaving my jacket at school. She knew there was another story, the real story. Her plan was to allow a difficult circumstance to come into my life so that I would come to the end of self and confess the truth. What did she do? Every night that I came home without that jacket I had to spend one hour in a dark storage room. This room was connected to the carport. It was a large room filled with boxes, tools and junk. What did I do in there? I sat on my dads riding lawn mower. My prayer? "Lord, please don't let a camel cricket jump on me." This punishment may seem cruel but it was effective. I was eleven years old and scared of the dark and scared of bugs. For nearly one week, each night I spent one hour with my fears.

Finally, I broke down. I came to the end of self. My excuses were not being bought, my lies were sounding more ridiculous every time I spoke. I finally, cried out to my mom and said I'm sorry. I confessed the lies and told the truth. When I cried out to my mom, she forgave me and delivered me. The truth had set me free.

Sin leads to desperation and despair. Sin snowballs into an avalanche of trouble. God allows the circumstances to occur so that we will come to the conclusion that enough is enough. The difficulties humble us and point us toward God. Ultimately, God's desire is for you and I to cry out to Him. Admitting sin, and confessing our need for God is the crucial step that leads a person to salvation and deliverance.

Here in Judges 6:6 we hear the Israelites crying out to God for deliverance. Will God save them? Yes. Romans 10:13 says, *"Whoever calls on the name of the Lord shall be saved".*

So, let me ask you, have you cried out to God lately? The children of Israel had come to the end of their rope, have you? That problem that you're trying to handle, have you turned it over to God? Have you called on His name? Have you cried out and said, "Lord, save me"?

If not, maybe you're not so sure you have a need. If that's the case, help is on the way. The next chapter helps you and I see our need.

Chapter Three

The Conviction
———————

Judges 6:7-10, NKJV

"And when it came to pass, when the children of Israel cried out to the Lord because of the Midianites, that the Lord sent a prophet to the children of Israel, who said to them, "I brought you up from Egypt and brought you out of the house of bondage; and I delivered you out of the hand of the Egyptians and out of the hand of all who oppressed you, and drove them out before you and gave you their land. Also I said to you, "I am the Lord your God; do not fear the gods of the Amorites, in whose land you dwell." "But you have not obeyed My voice."

The Lord convicts Israel of their sin. He speaks through a prophet and says, "you have not obeyed My voice". Was God upset? Yes. Did God have a rite to be upset? Yes. Delivering the children of Israel out of 400 years of bondage was no small task. In fact, God did it in such a fashion that generation after generation should have remembered this mighty act of God. Sadly, Gods people did forget about Him and began worshipping and fearing false gods.

God is the same yesterday, today and tomorrow. Our God is a jealous God. He doesn't want anyone or anything to occupy His position in your life. God didn't like it in Gideon's day and doesn't like it today. God doesn't like leftovers. God doesn't like riding in the backseat. God doesn't like hanging around in the background of your life. God wants to occupy the most important part of your life, your heart, the very center of who you are. There's only room for one person to sit on the throne of your life, you or God. If you choose to be in charge, He will allow circumstances to come into your life that will prove that you need Him in the drivers seat. What am I talking about? God will make Himself known through circumstances and through speaking to you about your life. He will go to great extremes to communicate the error of a person's ways. The term for this righteous pursuit is old-fashioned conviction.

In our text the Lord speaks to His people through a prophet. The prophet speaks a word of conviction and says, "You have disobeyed Gods voice". When you think about it the prophet said, "you've went against God's Word". God had warned His people of the threat of embracing other nations and their gods. In Leviticus chapter 26 the Lord warned His people that if they worship false gods and disobey His commands then they could expect tribulation and judgment. He warned that their enemies would overtake them and abuse them.

Here in Judges chapter six we see that the Midianites have steam rolled the Israelites. Who allowed this tribulation? God. Why? His people disobeyed His word. As a result of disobedience, which is sin, the children of Israel have a great need. They have a need for deliverance. They have cried out to God and said, "Lord, we need you". Now, a prophet has been sent by the Lord to convict and inform them of the magnitude of their sin. Just saying your sorry isn't enough. A child sometimes says they are sorry, only because they got caught.

A criminal will sometimes say he is sorry, only because he got caught. God is looking for genuine repentance among His people. He convicts them of their sin, in order that they might despise their own actions. Friend, God convicts you and I of sin, not only to inform us, but also to transform us. God's convicting power will make a person feel sick about what they have done, in order to straighten the path of the future.

Conviction is a subject that is rarely spoken of in Christian circles. Like the word repentance, conviction seems to be a negative word. Why? Because when a person is convicted they have been declared guilty. A sin has taken place and today no one wants to admit guilt or sin. In fact, we live in a day in which Gods' own people consistently try to justify sin. What have we done? The same thing as Israel in Gideon's day, we have disobeyed Gods' word.

Interestingly, when a person gets tired of sin and its bondage, and sees their need for God, they cry out to God and then He convicts them of their sin. He let's a person know that He is holy and they are sinful, thus conviction takes place. Here again, is the God given progression of events that lead to salvation.
1. Sin oppresses, devastates and leaves a person helpless.
2. Suddenly, the person gets tired of living this way, sees their need for change and cries out to God. Their plea, "Lord help me".
3. God in turn convicts the person of their sin and disobedience.

Friend, people in general do not like step three. They want to get saved without any conviction of sin. True conversion can only take place when a person calls out to God as a result of the conviction of sin. If a person's not convicted of their sin and their need to be saved, then salvation will not occur at that time. God convicts us of sin by the power of His Holy Spirit. The Holy Spirit draws us to the point of decision.

In our text, Israel was convicted of their sin. The prophet told them the reason God had allowed the Midianites to overtake them. They were reminded of God's word that had been passed down from generation to generation. The children of Israel were convicted of their sin and their need for deliverance.

Do you see the natural progression?

The Need - for deliverance from their enemies, to be saved from oppression and destruction.
The Cry - to God for help, the realization that only God can change things.
The Conviction - of present and past sin, the very reason for the difficult circumstances.

That all sounds like bad news, how could any of that lead to something good? This turn of events for the children of Israel leads them to only one way out. One hope. The hope of a savior, the hope of a deliverer, someone that could conquer their enemies. Good news is on the way. A savior awaits the turn of the page!

Chapter Four
The Savior Provided

Judges 6:11-14, NKJV

"Now the Angel of the Lord came and sat under the terebinth tree which was in Ophrah, which belonged to Joash the Abiezrite, while his son Gideon threshed wheat in the winepress, in order to hide it from the Midianites. And the Angel of the Lord appeared to him, and said to him, "The Lord is with you, you mighty man of valor!" Gideon said to Him, "O my Lord, if the Lord is with us, why then has all this happened to us? And where are all His miracles, which our fathers told us about, saying, "Did not the Lord bring us up from Egypt? But now the Lord has forsaken us and delivered us into the hands of the Midianites." Then the Lord turned to him and said, "Go in this might of yours, and you shall save Israel from the hand of the Midianites. Have I not sent you?"

We've seen the need, the cry, and the conviction and now we see God providing a savior. God was going to send Gideon to deliver His people by His power. But why Gideon? Why not someone else? Surely there was someone more qualified to lead the people. Was Gideon a leader when the Angel of the Lord visited him? No. But with the grace of God upon his life Gideon throughout chapters six and seven would be transformed into one of the Old Testaments greatest leaders.

Isn't it amazing how your life can change in an instant? How the direction of your life can be altered within the blink of an eye? Think about it, a tragic car accident can leave a person paralyzed for life, surviving a heart attack can change your eating habits forever, the words "it's a baby girl" instantly changes a father's life. For Gideon, it was the words of an angel sitting under a tree. The words, "go save Israel" changed Gideon's life forever.

As we look at Gideon do we see a person that's brave and courageous? Do we see a proven warrior? No. In scripture we see a man that's ordinary, in fact, we see a man that's afraid of the Midianites. He is a man that's oppressed and afraid, just like everyone else in his tribe. His tribe? The tribe of Manasseh was the least of the tribes of Israel, an unlikely tribe to produce a savior. God had a different opinion.

God sees Gideon threshing wheat in a winepress. God sees a man that is afraid and is hiding from the enemy. The custom of that time period reveals how afraid and intimidated Gideon had become. A winepress was constructed at the bottom of a hill, in a valley. During harvest time, the workers would gather the fruit of the vine in bushels and carry them down the hill to the winepress. Why is this significant? Gideon wasn't pressing grapes into wine, Gideon was threshing wheat. Normally, you would thresh wheat out in the open, sometimes on a hilltop. As you throw the wheat into the air, the wind separates the wheat from the chaff. But Gideon's not on a hilltop or out in the open field, he's down in the valley hiding in the winepress. God sees a weak and fearful Gideon.

God is sovereign. He knows what lies ahead. He doesn't just see you as you are today, God sees your potential. He looks at each of us and considers our future with Him at the wheel. Most great leaders didn't start out brave, confident or strong. God normally places these qualities and characteristics within a person. He develops them into a vessel that He can use for His glory and His purpose. God molded Gideon into a deliverer, a savior for His people. When the Angel of the Lord said, "you mighty man of valor", he was speaking of the future not the present. When God called me to preach, He called me preacher before I ever gave my first sermon. He called me a pastor before I came to Rocky Valley Baptist Church. God looks ahead, sees who we will become and then tells us who we are.

In Gideon's life God was calling the foolish to confound the wise, the weak to put to shame the things that are mighty, and the base things to bring down the lofty. Why you ask? Why doesn't God choose those that are the brightest, strongest or able? Because God is after one thing and one thing alone, glory. When the world sees God do the extraordinary through the life of an ordinary person, He receives glory and honor. The world's conclusion, God must be real.

Today, you may be thinking, "How can God use me? or "I am just ordinary, why would God choose to use me?" Maybe you're afraid and feel to weak to be used by God. If so, guess what? You're a candidate. In fact, God can use a person like you easier than He can use a know it all, or a person that thinks they have it all figured out.

Gideon was overwhelmed with what he had heard from the angel. Gideon didn't see himself as a leader or warrior, much less a deliverer and savior. During this period of time, God chooses Gideon to save His people from oppression and devastation.

For us, God sent a savior to save us from the oppression of sin and its devastating deathblow. God sent an unlikely candidate, a lamb, Jesus Christ. By the world's standards Jesus was weak and lowly. By God's standard, Jesus was the only sacrifice that could be made. Why? His only begotten son was blameless, sinless and righteous. Later in this book we see Gideon lead God's people to victory and freedom. This display of victory is only one example among many in scripture that foreshadows Jesus dieing on the cross for our sin, giving us victory over the oppression of sin, death and the grave. Once again, I want you to see the progression of our scripture:

The Need-man had a need to be delivered from oppression, a need to be saved.
The Cry- through difficult circumstances man cries out to the Lord for help.
The Conviction- God says you've sinned against me and need to repent.
The Savior Provided- God provides a savior to those who turn to Him and call upon His name.

The good news of the gospel is that God has provided a savior for mankind. His name is Jesus Christ. Jesus gave His life as a sacrifice for our sins. By His power a person can be set free from the oppression of sin and the sting of death. By His mercy that same person can be forgiven of sin and empowered to live a new life, a life of service for the Lord. Are you living this life? Has your life been instantly and eternally changed by the power of Jesus Christ? In the blink of an eye, the moment a person places their faith in Christ, life changes. The reason, God has provided a savior and a new purpose for that person's life. Gideon's life was forever changed through his encounter with God. If you've never accepted God's invitation to salvation, what's holding you back? Invite Jesus Christ to come into your life today and save you. God's provided a savior as well as this opportunity to respond by faith.

The question for Gideon was this, "will God deliver and make good on his promise?" The answer is yes, God is faithful. You may be asking this same question, can you trust God with your sin? Your future? Your problems? Your career? Your family? The answer is yes, He is trustworthy and able to care for you and empower you to live a life of victory.

God provided a savior for His people Israel, now we will see that deliverance is in His hands and on His radar. Deliverance is coming soon!

Chapter 5

The Deliverance Promised

Judges 6:15-16, NKJV

"So he said to Him, "O my Lord, how can I save Israel? Indeed my clan is the weakest in Manasseh, and I am the least in my father's house." And the Lord said to him, "Surely I will be with you, and you shall defeat the Midianites as one man."

Have you ever noticed throughout the bible that most of God's chosen vessels start out giving God excuses? Every nominating committee in every church should take comfort in the fact that even God gets excuses from His own people. Familiar statements like, "I can't", "I'll pray about it and get back with you"(and never do), or "there must be someone else that can do the job." Gideon pleads his case before the Lord and says, "I'm weak and I'm the least likely to succeed". God's reply, "I'll be with you and you will defeat the Midianites". God promises victory over the enemy and deliverance for His people.

Which brings us to an all-important question. What is a promise? Webster says a promise is to give assurance, or to agree to do or not do something. It's an agreement wrapped in trust either spoken or written. We are familiar with promises because we make them all the time. Notice, I said we make them all the time I didn't say we keep them all the time. The reason we fail to keep all of our promises is because of this fallen nature that we have inherited from Adam and Eve. There are times we really try to keep our promises but we forget or we loose track of time. Next thing you know, you have a broken promise. Fortunately most of the promises that we fail to keep are not life threatening, and usually are forgiven by the other person. God however, never forgets what He has promised nor will He loose track of time or get too busy to fulfill His obligation. God keeps His promises; in fact He is the only one that really bats a thousand when it comes to this area. If God has promised something He will deliver on that promise. Not to mention, on time, in His time.

In verse 16 God promises Gideon that He will deliver His people from the oppression of the Midianites. His promise, "surely, I will be with you, and you shall defeat the Midianites as one man." That word "surely" in the original text means assuredly, certainly and doubtless. The bottom line, God says you can count on it.

Throughout God's Word there are many promises made by God to you the reader. God promises things such as eternal life for those that believe, comfort for those that are hurting and help in our times of need. God has made many promises to us and many books have been written about this subject. God is more than just a promise maker, God is a promise keeper. Unlike fallen man, God is perfect. If he promises us something we can bank on it. Gideon was promised two things, God's active presence and God's deliverance.

First, God promised that He would be with Gideon. This presence of God later on would prove to be crucial considering

Gideon knew nothing about warfare or leading people. Gideon was the average Joe, he was ordinary, but with God's promised presence Gideon would become an extraordinary leader among God's people. Imagine that, an ordinary man living an extraordinary life.

   An ordinary life plus the presence of God can lead to some incredible results. Results such as:
- A massive boat constructed to save the human race and animal life. (Genesis chapers 6-8)
- The destruction of Pharaoh's empire. (Exodus ch. 5-12)
- The parting of the Red Sea. (Exodus 14:21-22)
- A miraculous water drenched sacrifice made on Mt. Carmel. (1 Kings ch. 18)
- Thousands of souls added to the kingdom. (Acts 2:41)

   God's promise of His presence would prove to be the greatest asset to Gideon. Today, do you consider the Lord's presence in your life the greatest asset that you have? Do you understand how important His power upon your life really is? This promise of His presence is made to all that call upon His name for salvation. Every person that comes to faith in Christ is born again and is indwelled with the presence of the Holy Spirit, who happens to be God. His presence will help you overcome temptation, empower you with discernment, and fill your life with power that is hard to describe. But know this, when God makes you a promise He will keep His Word. And His promise to followers of Christ is His indwelling presence.

   Secondly, God promises Gideon victory over the enemy, the Midianites. God in a sense says, "your going to fight a battle and your going to win". Use your imagination for just a moment. What if you could know the outcome of events, even before they transpire? Imagine knowing who was going to win the Super Bowl or World Series, even before the season

starts! We would certainly abuse such a power. God, however, knows the outcome of this future battle with the Midianites. God has the power to make it happen just as He has promised. Again, this word "surely" applies to this second promise just as it did to the first. God says, "surely, certainly, without a doubt, you will defeat the Midianites." Sounds like God has it all under control? He does, He always has and always will be in control.
- Have you ever felt like you were procrastinating, or delaying for some unknown reason?
- Maybe someone treats you poorly and later you realize they were doing you a favor?

Could it be that God is in control more than we think? Can He move our heart in such a way that we could be cold or indifferent to someone? Can God literally keep us from doing something or taking the wrong step?

It was November of 1999. I was still supply preaching, praying about my family's future and visiting seminaries. I didn't know what God had in store for me; I was just trying to be faithful one day at a time. The dealership in which I worked was doing great, I was the service manager and I really enjoyed the employees that I supervised. I cared about them and was concerned about their future. As God was leading me into full time ministry I was praying about my own replacement at the shop. On many occasions I would start to walk into my bosses office to inform him that a search for my replacement needs to get underway. I would get half way to his office and chicken out, or so it seemed. This went on for weeks. I began to beat myself up about it. My thought, I have eaten so much chicken over the years, now I have finally turned in to one.

Finally, I woke up one morning, found my backbone and walked into my boss's office ready to talk about finding my replacement. By the way, have you ever done that before?

Asked your boss to find your replacement? A word to the wise, don't do it unless God has told you to. Well, God had told me to do the difficult, the surprise to me and my boss was that God had done the impossible. When I expressed my concerns to my boss, he looked at me in shock. He asked me two questions. He said, "Jason, how long have you worked for this dealership?" I said, "almost two years". Then he asked, "Do you know how many people have applied for the service managers position in those two years?" I said, "No, I haven't a clue". He said, "None". My boss went on to say, " In two years no one has ever applied for the service managers position, but this day, the day you walk into my office and tell me to find your replacement, I receive a resume". In fact, just five minutes before I walked into that office, my boss had just read that resume and it was lying on his desk between us. The resume looked as if it was waiting to be discussed. We instantly realized that God was involved. We called the young man and almost hired him over the phone. In his resume, he had mentioned that he had been praying about moving to Middle Tennessee from Missouri. His desire was to find a General Motors dealership located within an hours drive to Nashville.

Was I procrastinating all those times I chickened out? Was I in control of the situation or God? God was in control of the event. God had planned it all out and he knew the outcome. Proverbs 21:1 says, "**The king's heart is in the hand of the Lord, like the rivers of water; He turns it wherever He wishes."** God promised Gideon that he would be victorious against the Midianites because He knew that He was going to be in control of the events. A great deliverance was promised and God was going to make good on His word. God is truly in control more than we will ever know or understand. Our job is not to understand it all, but to trust God and believe that He will keep his promises.

Gideon looked forward to this deliverance that was promised. The Old Testament prophets looked forward to the greatest deliverance of all time. They were promised that a deliverer would come and deliver mankind from the power of sin, the oppression of sin and the penalty of sin. That promise was fulfilled when Jesus came to earth. His birth was foretold by the prophets and came to pass over two thousand years ago. Jesus lived over thirty-three years on this earth, and then He laid down His life on the cross for all of mankind's sin. A one-time sin offering that would deliver all who believe from the bondage and penalty of sin. God promised this deliverance and God made good on His promise. Jesus paid all of our sin debt.

Today, the church, the body of Christ, looks forward to another deliverance. Jesus has promised in John chapter 14 that He is coming back for us, to receive us unto Himself. The word church actually means, "those called out". When that day comes, followers of Christ will be called out and delivered out of this world. We will be delivered from the environment of sin that has spiraled down for centuries. Yes, the only one that can keep all promises has promised a great deliverance. That person is God Himself. God had promised Gideon and his people deliverance from their enemies, God has promised you and I the same thing. Do you believe Him? Do you trust God's Word? "Surely" He will keep His word. "Certainly" He will keep His word. "Without a Doubt" God will keep His word.

Reflecting back on this section of the book ask yourself these questions:
- **What "needs" do I have that can only be addressed by God?**
- **Have I come to the end of self and "cried" out to God for help?**

- **Do I understand why God brings "conviction" to my life?**
- **Do I know that a "savior" has been provided, and have I been "saved"?**
- **Do I truly trust God and believe that He will make good on His "promises"?**

Section Two

"God Blesses Those That Give"

Chapter Six
"The Offering Prepared"

Judges 6:17-19, NKJV

"Then he said to Him, "If now I have found favor in Your sight, then show me a sign that it is You who talk with me. "Do not depart from here, I pray, until I come to You and bring my offering and set it before You." And He said, I will wait until you come back." So Gideon went in and prepared a young goat, and unleavened bread from an ephah of flour. The meat he put in a basket, and he put the broth in a pot; and he brought them out to Him under the terebinth tree and presented them.

Have you ever felt like God was speaking to you, or guiding you into something but you weren't one hundred percent sure it was God that was doing the talking? You thought it was, but you had some doubt. Why did you have the doubt? Was it because the thing God told you to do seemed unreasonable or ridiculous? Did the message or task seem impossible? If your answer is yes to some of these questions then you may have heard from God. I've found that God doesn't just call us to do that which we can already accomplish. Most of the time there's an element of uncertainty, an element of the unknown, and friends, we don't like the unknown. We prefer all things to be spelled out for us, laid out for us and done for us most of the time. God normally doesn't operate the way we operate. His ways are higher than our ways and greater than our ways. In fact, if we had our way, we would not walk by faith at all. We would be sight walkers. We would see something and then believe it. Today, we constantly want to see something, we constantly desire to see proof.

Well Gideon, like us, wants to see some proof. Gideon is looking for a sign. He wants to know for sure that this angel has been sent from God. Gideon then proceeds to ask for a sign, a small sign indeed.

Gideon asks the angel to stay there while he goes to prepare an offering. Gideon says "show me this sign". The angel says, "I will wait until you come back". Gods' favor was certainly upon Gideon to ablige him this way. In a sense God waits while Gideon prepares an offering. By the way, what have you offered to God lately? Have you prepared an offering for the Lord? Maybe God is waiting on you to offer some of your time, energy and resources for His namesake?

Well, while the Angel of the Lord is waiting, Gideon is preparing an offering. Gideon prepares a young goat, he prepares some unleavened bread and he prepares some broth in a pot. Gideon is quite the host. When was the last time someone said to you, "sit down while I cook you some dinner"? Gideon was looking for a sign. He wanted to know for sure that this messenger was from God. So what does he do? He prepares an offering just in case this is truly God speaking to him. Friend, when God comes near to us, and he has, we all should make an offering to Him.

Obviously, Gods' favor was upon Gideon. God didn't just send an angel to anybody and everybody. This encounter with the Angel of the Lord was a big deal to Gideon. In fact, it was a life changing moment in time and a turning point in Gideon's life. God had spoken to him and was commissioning him.
    Friend, whenever God speaks to you it's a big deal. Don't ever consider it a small thing or a common thing. When a person hears from God the result should be a change in behavior, a change in direction and a change in the persons heart. Gideon knew that the presence of this angel was very significant. Gideon realized that the commission he had been given, to lead Gods' people in battle, was huge. That's why he wanted to be sure that this was God speaking to him. Gideon's motive was pure, he didn't want to put Gods' people into harms way unless God was truly calling the shots. Gideon wanted to be hospitable to this Angel of the Lord, but more than that he desired a sign from the Lord, a sign that would prove that this was God that was speaking to him and not someone else.
    Gideon's desire to know for sure the author of the message let's us know that someone else could have been speaking. But who? Who else could have been speaking to Gideon? Who else can speak to you and I other than God? There are at least three answers, the flesh, the world and Satan.
    First, let's talk about the flesh. You and I have a sinful nature. A nature that will continually try to appease the flesh, promote self and indulge in sinful behavior. The flesh looks out for itself and tries to control us by tapping into the thoughts that run through our mind. If the voice speaking to you is looking to take care of your fleshly needs and is looking to promote you and you alone, then your not hearing from God. When God is speaking to you the course that He instructs you to take

will always glorify Him, promote godliness and bless not only you, but others. Gideon was truly hearing from God, but at the same time his flesh was also speaking. While God was saying "you will win this battle with the Midianites", Gideon's flesh was saying "that can't be so, who me?" I have found that when God speaks, our flesh usually tries to put in it's two cents.

Secondly, the world speaks to us. The world says things like "do it, you don't have fun any more", or "try smoking, it will help calm your nerves", or "just one drink won't hurt you". The world has no problem speaking to us, in fact, the world is talking non-stop. How do you know when the world is talking to you? It's easy, measure the good that can come from the action it's asking you to take. The worlds' cure for you is very temporary. The worlds' voice always speaks in terms of quick fixes. The problem is this, we don't need a quick fix, we desperately need help every day. That kind of sustained help can only come from God. Here in Judges chapter six, the world needed help, but the world wasn't calling out to Gideon, God was calling.

Third, the old devil himself, Satan, speaks to us. Satan comes as a deceiver as an "angel of light" the bible declares. He whispers half truths to you and I all the time, and sometimes we buy into his lies. He will see the desires of our hearts, then he tempts us by enticing us to embrace our fleshly desires. Satan will not only use the world and the flesh to carry out his will, he will also use people. People that will mislead you by steering you out of Gods' will for your life. People that you may love and respect can even mislead you and be used by the devil. Gideon here in verse 17 is asking for a sign because he knows that this angel could be misleading him. Think about it, what if this angel had not been sent by God? What if sending Gideon into battle was a lie from the devil? What would be at stake? Gods' people would have been utterly destroyed.

This is why Gideon asks for a sign, this is why Gideon prepares an offering.

Friend, living in a fallen world, among fallen people, we must continually discern who is talking to us. Why? Because the flesh isn't going to just come out and say, "hey, if you take this drink, you'll probably become an alcoholic". The worlds not going to say, "hey, if you buy four more lottery tickets you'll probably lose your bank account gambling". Satan's not going to openly say, "hey, if you disobey God today, there will be consequences down the line". No, the flesh, the world and satan will lie to you, abuse you and leave you wounded.

Discernment needs to be a high priority in everyone's life. We need to discern who is talking to us. We need to know when it's God. By the way, how do you know when God is speaking to you? His voice sounds like His Word. But if a person is not reading and studying the Word of God they will not know it's God. They will usually question God.

Currently, as I am writing this book, I find myself at a cross roads. God has been speaking to me for months about moving me and my family. Even though the church I am serving is great, the people are great, the ministry has prospered, and the community in which we live is wonderful, God is still saying, "I am going to move you." After preparing me for a couple of months, God spoke to me on December 13th and said, "you will be at Upper Helton Baptist Church in February". God had me saying, "yes, I will go" before He ever told me the "where". After sharing this news with my wife, she revealed that God had also been speaking to her for several months. The same was true for our mothers, they both knew God was about to move our family. Through other signs and wonders God confirmed His plans for our family. God had spoken.

I would like to say that the flesh was silent, but it wasn't. Early on, my mind kept saying, "why?" I began to reason things out in my head, all the while God kept saying, " I'm moving you". The flesh wanted to stay at Rocky Valley Baptist Church. Staying would have been predictable, comfortable and secure. The flesh really had a hard time with this word from God, but Gods' voice prevailed. Satan wasn't going to let it go either. The funny thing about Satan is this, he didn't mind me staying at Rocky Valley and preaching because he knew I would be out of Gods will and into his will. Have you ever realized that Satan has a will for your life? Satans will for your life will lead you to disaster. During this period of time in my life, there were a few people that would have led me astray if I had listened to them. People that meant well, but unfortunately were wrong. I had to make a choice. Was I going to listen to my flesh, the world, Satan or God? I chose to listen to God. What God was calling me to do, glorified Him, required faith and would not only advance His kingdom but would grow me as a pastor. God wanted me to be sure and I was certain of His call.

Gideon wanted to be sure this was God. So Gideon prepares this meal as a sign. By the way, this meal was no ordinary meal. Notice in verse 19, concerning the offering our text says, "he presented them". Gideon presented the meal. When you study the word "presented" you find that the root of this word is a Hebrew word "Nagash". Nagash is a word used to describe the posture of the priest as he would bring a sacrifice or offering to the Lord. This was no ordinary meal that Gideon had prepared this was truly an offering. This young goat was presented as a meat offering and the broth was presented as a drink offering. In the Old Testament when this word presented is used in conjunction with sacrificial offerings, the priest would have the right posture and the right attitude. The priest would offer the sacrifice with respect and reverence. Gideon in verse 19 presented this offering that he had prepared in the right way. He humbly came before the Angel of the Lord and presented his offering.

When you and I make an offering, a sacrifice or return the tithe unto God, we must have the right posture. We must have a heart that is right with God. In our churches, the time of offering is usually a time of dread for some people instead of a time of reverence to God. If you and I sacrifice our time, energy and resources with the wrong attitude then the offering we have made is for nothing. If our heart is not right, then the offering we prepare will not satisfy us or God. If we begrudgingly give to Gods' work we will not feel a sense of purpose. God is looking for us to not only tithe, give one tenth of our income for his kingdoms' work, but to give an offering of our time as well. In fact, everything we give to God needs to be given with the right attitude.

Gideon did just that, he presented this offering to the Angel of the Lord respectfully. This was much more than a sign, this was also an act of worship. The very fact that the angel stayed was confirmation alone.

Remember, Gideon at first was seeking proof thru this meal, now he is in a state of worship. Shouldn't that be the case with us, that we worship God when we realize that He is who He says He is?

In this chapter, Gideon was looking for a sign as he prepared a meal. He sacrificed and made an offering unto God. Keep reading and discover that God blesses those that give to Him.

Chapter Seven

"The Miracle Performed"

Judges 6:20-24, NKJV

"The Angel of God said to him, "Take the meat and the unleavened bread and lay them on this rock, and pour out the broth." And he did so. Then the Angel of the Lord put out the end of the staff that was in His hand, and touched the meat and the unleavened bread; and fire rose out of the rock and consumed the meat and the unleavened bread. And the Angel of the Lord departed out of his sight. Now Gideon perceived that He was the Angel of the Lord, so Gideon said, "Alas, O Lord God! For I have seen the Angel of the Lord face to face." Then the Lord said to him, "Peace be with you; do not fear, you shall not die." So Gideon built an altar there to the Lord, and called it The Lord Is Peace. To this day it is still in Ophrah of the Abiezrites.

Here we see the miracle performed. Remember, this was a test, Gideon was looking for proof. If the Angel of the Lord was to consume this food by fire, then Gideon would know this was God speaking to him and that God had accepted this food as a meat and drink offering. If the Angel had simply eaten the food, then Gideon would have known that this Angel wasn't from God.

As you look back into Genesis you will find that Abraham was visited by the Angel of the Lord. Abraham, like Gideon, prepared a meal for the Angel as well. But something very different took place. The Angel of the Lord ate Abraham's food but here in Judges six the Angel of the Lord consumes the food with fire. Why? Why would the Angel of the Lord eat Abraham's food and not Gideon's? The answer is simple. The motives of the two men were completely different. Abraham knew this Angel was sent from God, so he, out of respect, shows hospitality. Gideon presented the food as a test and as an offering. God knew the motives of these two men. He knew the reason they were presenting Him with the food.

There's a lesson in this for us. God knows our heart. He knows when you and I give out of obedience, sincerity and devotion to Him. He also knows when we begrudgingly give or give to Him with strings attached. Have you ever noticed how small a $20 bill looks at Walmart, but how big a $20 bill looks in the offering plate. Sometimes we are willing to blow money, while we are afraid to give money to the Lord and His work.

God blesses the giver when his heart is right and when there are no strings attached. God truly blesses us when we show Him respect and return to Him that which is already His.

Well, Gideon gives this offering to the Angel of the Lord and the Angel consumes the offering with fire. What did Gideon learn from these turn of events? He learned that this angel was truly sent from God and that God indeed was calling him to lead God's people into battle against the Midianites. Gideon asked for a sign, prepared an offering and the Lord performed the miracle.

Did you notice that the Angel of the Lord disappears as Gideon receives his confirmation? I have discovered that God deals with us in similar fashion. Sometimes after hearing from God and receiving confirmation on a project, a direction or program, God will sometimes become silent for a period of time. Why? Why would God seemingly disappear after giving us confirmation? The answer, He wants to see if you and I will walk by faith. I believe He sometimes sits back and watches us to see if we will act upon that which He has told us. Isn't that walking by faith? Yes. Walking by faith is taking God at His word and putting His word into action. The Apostle James said that faith without works is dead. I happen to agree. If a person believes God wants them to change jobs, then guess what? That person needs to be working on their resume and start prayerfully applying for other jobs. Some people want God to just drop things out of the sky. They hear from God but then they fail to act upon the word they have heard. Walking by faith is taking steps toward what God has said, small steps at times, but steps nevertheless.

    Well, Gideon hears from this angel and believes that this angel was sent from God. His response to the miracle performed and the angel's disappearance in verse 22 reveals that not only did Gideon believe the angel was sent from God, he also feared for his life. Gideon had seen the Angel of the Lord face to face. Scripture says that it is a fearful thing to fall into the hands of a holy God. Gideon realized that he had been in the presence of holiness.

    But notice, although the Angel had disappeared out of sight, the Angel speaks to Gideon. The Angels words, "Peace be with you; do not fear, you shall not die." Now friend, that's true peace when God tells you that you will not die! Listen, if you have put your faith and trust in Jesus Christ as your personal Lord and Savior, God has whispered the same sentiment to you, "peace be with you, don't fear; you will not die." God has promised eternal life to all that believe upon His Son Jesus Christ. In John 11:25 Martha the sister of Lazarus was grieving the death of her brother when Jesus says to her, "*I am the resurrection and the life, He who believes in Me, though he may die, he shall live. And whoever lives and believes in Me shall never die. Do you believe this?*" Jesus asks Martha do you believe what I have just told you, she responds one verse later and says "yes, I believe".

Gideon was comforted by the Angel's promise. Friend, when God makes you a promise you can take it to the bank. He has the ability to back up His words.

In this chapter, Gideon presents an offering to the Angel of the Lord. The Angel performs the miracle and consumes the offering. The Angel then disappears. Gideon then receives his confirmation and fearfully cries out, then we see the Angel calm Gideon's fears. Would these miracles have been performed if Gideon had not presented an offering? Would Gideon have received his confirmation to lead God's people if he had not been faithful to discern the author of this conversation? I have found that if you and I do the difficult, He will do the impossible. If you and I will offer ourselves to Him, He will not only give us confirmation but perform miracles as well. Many people fail to see miracles in their personal lives because they choose to walk by sight. God wants you to see the "Gideon in You", but it's going to require faith on your part. You've got to believe that God is calling you to do great things for His kingdom. When you walk by faith and believe God is calling you, get ready for a test. Gideon had given God a test and God passed the test and gave Gideon a sign. Gideon now believes that God is calling him to lead the people into battle against the Midianites. God is now poised to test Gideon. Why? The next section reveals that God tests those He calls.

Section Three

"God Tests Those He Calls"

Chapter Eight

"Why A Test?"
_____

Judges 6:25-32, NKJV

"Now it came to pass the same night that the Lord said to him, "Take your father's young bull, the second bull of seven years old, and tear down the altar of Baal that your father has, and cut down the wooden image that is beside it; 'and build an altar to the Lord your God on top of this rock in the proper arrangement, and take the second bull and offer a burnt sacrifice with the wood of the image which you shall cut down."

"So Gideon took ten men from among his servants and did as the Lord had said to him. But because He feared his father's household and the men of the city too much to do it by day, he did it by night. And when the men of the city arose early in the morning, there was the altar of Baal, torn down; and the wooden image that was beside it was cut down, and the second bull was being offered on the altar which had been built. So they said to one another, "who has done this thing?" And when they had inquired and asked, they said, "Gideon the son of Joash has done this thing."

Then the men of the city said to Joash, "Bring out your son, that he may die, because he has torn down the altar of Baal, and because he has cut down the wooden image that was beside it." But Joash said to all who stood against him, "Would you plead for Baal? Would you serve him? Let the one who would plead for him be put to death by morning! If he is a god, let him plead for himself, because his altar has been torn down!"

Wow! That my friend, was a test. The same night that the Angel of the Lord tells Gideon "peace be with you; do not fear, you shall not die" the Lord has Gideon risk his own life. What was God teaching Gideon? A great spiritual truth, walking by faith and taking risks go hand in hand. God prepares us to do his will. God tests those he calls.

Israel had a great need, a need for deliverance. For deliverance to take place, a deliverer must be sent. In order for a deliverer to be sent, a deliverer must be prepared or developed. That's where Gideon comes into the picture. God calls Gideon to deliver His people, but before Gideon could lead He had to be tested. Gods' goal was to mold Gideon into a leader. Again, God tests those He calls.

Before we go any further, let's define the word test. A test puts something or someone through an examination in order to find proof. A Physician will order several tests upon his patient in order to prove that their sickness is due to a virus or bacteria. A school teacher will give a pop quiz and test her students knowledge in order to prove that learning is taking place. A person must pass a driving test in order to obtain a driver's license. In all of these cases, the test gives proof.

In Gideon's case, Gods' test would prove Gideon's character or lack of character. When testing something you examine the subject closely. God put Gideon through some tests. God examined Gideon closely. Gideon's heart was under the microscope. God wanted to know if He could depend on Gideon to be the leader of His people.

I don't know about you, but I don't like tests. In school, I was terrified of tests. The reason? I didn't like to study. The tests however, would reveal the truth about my study habits and how much I had learned. Tests from God are very similar. God will test those he calls in order to reveal strengths and weaknesses.

A ship for instance is tested greatly before it is sent out to sea. The engine, the buoyancy and the crew are all tested prior to service. Whatever God is calling you to do, He too, will put you through some tests. He will test your will, your heart, your commitment and most importantly your allegiance to Him. Testing is needed.

Gideon is called by God to deliver the Israelites from the oppression of the Midianites. God is calling Gideon to take a stand and lead His nation into battle. So God gives Gideon a test before He sends Him out, a test to see if Gideon would fear God more than man.

Before I became the pastor of my first church God put me through several tests. God tested me to see if I would lay down old habits and pick up new habits. He tested me to see if I would take a stand for Him at my work, If I would go places that he told me to go. He tested me to see if I would leave my career and follow Him. Then as I began to preach He tested me to see if I would be patient and wait for His opportunity. The tests went on and on, guess what? I am still tested by God. Why? Because God tests those He calls.

As a follower of Jesus Christ, there are things that God calls us to do. And to find out where we stand, God will test us. In fact, our faith will be on trial. God tests our faith to see if we will obey Him. Gideon in our text was tested by God. He was given two assignments by God. The first assignment was one of destruction. As you turn the page, let's see how Gideon deals with God's assignment and how fearing God is more important than fearing man.

Chapter Nine

"Gideon's First Assignment - One Of Destruction"

Judges 6:25

"Now it came to pass the same night that the Lord said to him, "Take your father's young bull, the second bull of seven years old, and tear down the altar of Baal that your father has, and cut down the wooden image that is beside it;"

This has been a long day for Gideon. In this one day, God has called Gideon to serve Him, God has revealed Himself to Gideon through signs and wonders, and now God is putting Gideon through his first test. The test is to destroy the altar of Baal. God is testing the will of Gideon.

Baal was a false god, a Canaanite god in fact. And here we see that the Israelites had been offering sacrifices to this false god. This is the sin that caused God to deliver the Israelites into the hands of the Midianites. The Israelites had drifted far away from Jehovah God, the one true living God. They were worshipping false gods and Gideon's father had the responsibility of caring for the altar. Destroying this altar would take great courage on the part of Gideon. It would also be a test of his allegiance. Would Gideon dare take a stand against the status quo? Would Gideon risk damaging his relationship with his father? The answer, yes. And later we see that Gideon carries out this task at night. Why at night you ask? Gideon, like you and I, was sometimes afraid.

God puts Gideon through this test in order to develop courage and increase Gideon's faith. If Gideon was going to battle the Midianites he was going to need a boat load of courage and a super size order of faith to go with it. This test, this first assignment would be the vehicle God would use to strengthen Gideon.

What about us? How does God strengthen our lives and increase our faith? The same way He strengthened Gideon, through tests and trials. We may not be called to tear down an altar of a false god, but God may test you and I to see if we will lay down an old habit, a bad friend, or leave a job that's a dead end. God will test you and I to see if we are going to listen to Him. God sometimes gives us small tests and then greater tests as we walk with Him.

One of the greatest examples we have in scripture is young David. Before David had slain Goliath with a sling and a stone, he was tested with a bear and a lion. David was a shepherd. His job was to protect and care for the flock. To protect the sheep, David had to kill predators like bears and lions. And by the way, he did it when no one was looking, in utter obscurity. David time and again passed various tests that ultimately led to one of his greatest battles, the battle with Goliath. David defeated Goliath and later became King.

How important were those tests out in the pasture, those tests in obscurity? They were extremely important for the devolvement of young David the future King. David could be trusted to defend the sheep and the nation of Israel. He did both well, but not without some testing and trials.

Often times God will test a person first in obscurity, then publicly. God will sometimes test you and I to see if we will do the right thing when no one is looking, when an audience can't be found.

Gideon was tested by God to see if he would go public with what God had said privately. And in the middle of this test is a question of allegiance. Would Gideon risk losing his relationship with his father over God's command? Would Gideon have to stand up against his father over what God had commanded him to do? Yes. Why do you think this was important to God? The answer can be found in Matthew 10:37-38, Jesus said, "He who loves father or mother more than Me is not worthy of Me. And he who loves son or daughter more than Me is not worthy of Me." "And he who does not take his cross and follow after me is not worthy of me." Those are some strong words from Jesus and they apply to Gideon in this first test.

Listen, if Gideon is unwilling to stand for God at home, how will he face the Midianites. Likewise, if you and I are unwilling to stand for God in our home, how are we going to take a stand for righteousness in a world that wants to chew us up and spit us out? God's desire for every believer is for them to stand on His word with courage and faith. And just as God develops these characteristics in Gideon, God also seeks to develop these characteristics in us. With that said, we need to accept the fact that God's development process involves tests and trials.

The title of this book "The Gideon in You" suggests that anyone can serve God, live for God, and be used by God. For that to take place, a transformation must take place as well. A change must occur, the characteristics of God must be developed in us, tests and trials must come. Gideon passed his first assignment, he destroyed the altar of Baal. Now, it's time to move on to the next assignment, one of construction. Gideon is realizing what you and I must realize, that walking with God is a progression, there's always a task at hand.

Chapter Ten

"Gideon's Second Assignment - One of Construction"

Judges 6:26-27

"and build an altar to the Lord your God on top of this rock in the proper arrangement, and take the second bull and offer a burnt sacrifice with the wood of the image which you shall cut down." So Gideon took ten men from among his servants and did as the Lord said to him. But because he feared his father's household and the men of the city too much to do it by day, he did it by night."

Gideon's first assignment was one of destruction, his second assignment was one of construction. God instructed Gideon to build a new altar and sacrifice the bull before Him. God says, "you'll need some wood so cut up the graven image of Baal and use this wood to build a fire." Have you ever noticed, that walking with God and doing as God commands, will sometimes get you into trouble with society? Gideon has not only torn down the image of this false god, now he is going to have to burn the pieces. You know, God doesn't do anything half way. It's all the way or nothing with God. You are either saved or lost, for Him or against Him, there's no straddling the fence with God.

Gideon was obedient he burned the pieces of this destroyed wooden image of Baal. You know what? In the end God will burn up anything and everything that's false in this world. This image of Baal just got it's turn a little early!

In verse 27 we see Gideon carry out both assignments, he obeyed the Lord's command. That must have been refreshing to God, to have an Israelite obey his voice for a change. Gideon tears down the old altar, destroys the image of Baal, builds the new altar and sacrifices the bull to the Lord. Kind of, out with the old and in with the new! God is still in the business of renewal.

- **God tears down with the intent to rebuild.**
- God had Gideon tear down a hopeless altar to a false god in order to build a hope filled altar to the one true living God.
- **God tears down with the intent to rebuild.**
- God will allow a hopeless life to crumble (a life built on sin and self) in order to give that person true hope built on His Son Jesus Christ the solid rock.
- **God tears down with the intent to rebuild.**
- God will sometimes allow a person to drift aimlessly for a while so that they may finally turn to Him and head in His direction.
- **God tears down with the intent to rebuild.**
- A lost person goes from being hopelessly destroyed by sin, to being gloriously saved by grace. From being the old man in the flesh, to being a new creature in Christ.
- **God tears down with the intent to rebuild.**

This wasn't a new thing for God to do. In fact, He often destroys and then rebuilds. Take Noah and the flood in Genesis chapters 6 & 7, man was continually bent toward sin. Therefore, God brought judgment and destroyed the earth with a flood. The only people that were saved were Noah and his family. Noah builds an ark, a huge boat. The ark becomes their savior and petting zoo all at the same time. The flood comes and destroys the earth then God rebuilds the earth once again. In a sense the earth was born again.

God does the same thing with people. God will sometimes allow a person to hit rock bottom so that they will turn to Him, repent, and allow Him to rebuild their life.

Do you see that with Gideon? Gideon is tested by God to tear down his fathers' altar to a false god, and rebuild an altar to the one true living God. It was a chance to start over, an opportunity to walk with God once again.

Well, Gideon passed the test, he feared God more than Joash his earthly father. And through this test God begins to develop courage and faith in Gideon. But what about the towns people? What was the reaction of the people? Turn the page and watch how God will bless you when you stand for Him!

Chapter Eleven
"Passing the Test = Blessing"

Judges 6:28-32

"And when the men of the city arose early in the morning, there was the altar of Baal, torn down; and the wooden image that was beside it was cut down, and the second bull was being offered on the altar which had been built. So they said to one another, "Who has done this thing?" And when they had inquired and asked, they said, "Gideon the son of Joash has done this thing."

Then the men of the city said to Joash, "Bring out your son, that he may die, because he has torn down the altar of Baal, and because he has cut down the wooden image that was beside it." But Joash said to all who stood against him, "would you plead for Baal? Would you save Him? Let the one who would plead for him be put to death by morning! If he is god, let him plead for himself, because his altar has been torn down!" Therefore on that day he called him Jerubbaal, saying, "Let Baal plead against him, because he has torn down his altar."

Here we see the reaction of the people. The people see that the old altar to Baal is torn down, they also see that the graven image of wood has been chopped to pieces. They also notice a new altar has been built and a bull is being sacrificed even as they speak. What did the people do next? They play a game of "who did it". They ask one another, who did this thing? Finally, they conclude that Gideon the son of Joash is responsible. Their response was predictable; they want to give Gideon the death sentence. Today, the death sentence takes years before it is a reality for a person on death row. In Gideon's day, the death sentence could be carried out in minutes. So, Gideon's life is in real danger.

While the people's response is predictable, the response of Joash, Gideon's father is unpredictable. Joash uses some discernment and wisdom. He concludes that if Baal was really a god, then Baal should have defended himself. Joash then defends his son Gideon. Joash challenges the people to turn against Baal and they follow his lead.

Gideon passes the test and is obedient to Gods command. His reward is influence among God's people. Friend, when you stand for God He will bless you with influence, favor and added responsibility. When Gideon fired up that new altar and smoked that graven image of Baal, he was on his way to becoming the servant that God desired. God's favor was upon Gideon and the peoples plan to kill him was changed. Gideon passed the test and helped the people turn from their false gods all at the same time.

But his faith and courage would still need to grow. His dependence and trust in God would still need to increase. Gideon was faithfully progressing toward God's will for his life, a victorious life, one step at a time, one test at a time. Remember, a test puts someone or something through an examination in order to find proof.

Gideon passed the test and was blessed.
What test is God putting you through today?
What is He testing you for?
What characteristics is He developing in you?

A word of caution, don't run from the tests in life, learn from them. Allow God to develop his characteristics in you through yielding and obeying through the tests. God's goal is for you and I to be Christ-like, and tests are needed. Remember, God tests those he calls. And if you pass the test you will be blessed!

Section Four

"God Calls Us To Serve"

Chapter Twelve

The Goal Is Serving, Not Training

Judges 6:33-35, NKJV

"Then all the Midianites and Amalekites, the people of the East, gathered together; and they crossed over and encamped in the Valley of Jezreel. But the Spirit of the LORD came upon Gideon; then he blew the trumpet, and the Abiezrites gathered behind him. And sent messengers throughout all Manasseh, who also gathered behind him. He also sent messengers to Asher, Zebulun, and Naphtali; and they came up to meet them."

As a refresher, let's remember some important facts. The Midianites and the Amalekites are oppressing God's people, the Israelites. The Israelites call out to God for deliverance. God then calls Gideon to lead the people into battle. Gideon tested God to make sure that it was the Lord that was calling him, then God tested Gideon's faith. Gideon's faith was tested and as a result Gideon's courage and trust in God was increased. Gideon's father, Joash, as well as the townspeople put their trust in Gideon's leadership. Now it is time for Gideon to step into the role of commander, a military commander.

God had called Gideon to serve. Preparation was part of the process, but not the ultimate goal. Serving God was the goal. Today, God calls His children to serve. And even though testing, preparation and training are needed, they are not the goal. God trains us up in order to prove character, develop our skills and grow our faith. But there comes a time when God's children must step into the role that God has prepared. For example, Sunday school and discipleship training will prepare a Christian to serve God, but many Christians stay in this mode of training and never serve God. The goal is serving, not training.

I know of a man that repels over the edge of rock cliffs. He carefully ties the rope to a tree at the top of the cliff then he lowers himself down the face of the rock wall until he reaches the ground below. This man learns how to tie knots, he prepares and trains. But his goal is to repel down the face of the cliff, not to simply train. Preparation is needed, but preparation is not the goal.

In serving God, training and preparation are needed. We need to read our bibles, we need to know what God's word says and we need to be tested. That's all good, but we must take it a step further. God's children are called to serve Him. If we attend Sunday school and discipleship classes and never serve God then all we did was receive some training. Training and preparation are not the goal, serving God is the goal.

Here in Judges Chapter six the stage for the battle is being set. And while some preparation is still taking place in Gideon's life, God requires Gideon to step in as the leader. It's time for Gideon to serve. Here is a lesson that God's children need to grasp. Your life doesn't have to be perfect before you start serving God. Discipleship and growing in the Lord is a life long process. If you are waiting for the perfect time to serve

God it will never come. The time to serve God is today. Allow God to keep growing you spiritually, but serve Him today.

Are you serving God? Is serving God one of your goals in life? Are you making yourself available for God to use? Are you allowing God to train you up? Are you going through a test? Is God refining your character? Is God growing your faith?

Listen, serving God will bring you blessings, fulfillment, and joy. But beware, serving God will also bring attention to you. God's people will take notice and encourage you, but the devil will also take notice and put a bulls' eye on your back! As you turn the page, you'll discover that when you serve God you become a target.

Chapter Thirteen

"When You Serve, You Become A Target"

Judges 6:33, NKJV

"Then all the Midianites and Amalekites, the people of the East, gathered together; and they crossed over and encamped in the Valley of Jezreel"

When God's children serve Him the threat of the enemy becomes a startling reality. Most Christians believe that the devil is real. However, the fierceness of this enemy is truly revealed when they begin to serve God. As they serve they realize that their life has now become a target.

In Gideon's day the enemies were the people from the east. The Midianites and the Amalekites would come and go into this region at various times of the year. During harvest time, they would come in and raid the crops and wreak havoc, then they would retreat back over the Jordan river to their own land for a time.

So here in verse 33, the enemy once again comes over the Jordan River hoping to see God's people run like rabbits.

The enemy comes hoping to paralyze the Israelites with fear. The enemy comes assuming that the Israelites would bow in submission one more time.

Jesus in John 10:10 spoke of the devil and says, "The enemy comes to kill, steal and destroy". The enemy, Satan, comes toward us hoping to dominate our lives by fear and oppression. The threat of the enemy was real in Gideon's day and is real in our day.

The Midianites and Amalekites represent evil. They would come over the Jordan River and kill people, steal crops and destroy lives. For God's people, the threat of the enemy was very real. The Israelites knew they were out numbered by these wicked people from the east. The enemies' threat was real. And now because Gideon was willing to serve God, His life had become a target.

When God's children submit to God's leadership and serve Him, they become targets of the enemy. Satan will try to kill, steal and destroy their witness. And Satan knows that he can't steal someone's salvation, but he can steal that person's joy. The enemy will also try to assassinate your character and integrity as you serve God. His goal is to destroy your witness. Why? Because Satan doesn't want Gods children to reach this lost world for Christ. The enemies' threat is real.

Satan wants to discourage God's children from serving. He will distract you, he will tempt you, he will influence you with his arsenal. Arsenal, you ask? Yes, Arsenal. He will tempt you and I to indulge in watching television programs that are focused on sin. He will lure a person to visit websites that are inappropriate. Satan will appease the flesh when an attractive person walks by at your work. He will say things to you like, "hey, even a married man can look at another woman, looking is not a sin". And the list goes on and on. Friends, Satan is striving to destroy our witness. And when you serve

God, you can count on discouragement to come your way. Discouragement will even come from people that love you. When a person chooses to serve God they become a target of the enemy.

Gideon was a walking bulls' eye. God had tested Gideon and had trained him up for battle. God knew it, Gideon knew it, Gideon's father knew it, God's people knew it, and guess what? Satan knew it as well. And in verse 33, here comes the enemy one more time.

As you have read this chapter you might be thinking, "Why in the world would anyone want to serve God if they are going to become a target of the devil?" Listen, Gideon knew the threat was great. Gideon knew that the risk was high. But Gideon also knew that the same God that called him to lead would help him become victorious. Remember, if we are going to walk by faith, then we are going to have to be willing to take a risk. By the way, the bulls' eye that is placed on your back is really intended for God. Satan is not really mad at you, he is mad at God. God knows this and that's why He will reward those that willingly serve Him and suffer for Him.

Let me ask you a question. Are you a target of the enemy? Are you serving God? Do fiery darts whiz by your head? Do you find yourself embracing your armor even more? If you're serving God, keep up the good work, represent Him well, and trust in Him even more.

If you're not serving God, the next two chapters will hopefully inspire you to enlist and start wearing your bulls' eye. Remember, when you live for God you become a target.

Chapter Fourteen

"When You Serve, God Shows Up"

Judges 6:34-35, NKJV

"But the Spirit of the Lord came upon Gideon; then he blew the trumpet, and the Abiezrites gathered behind him. And he sent messengers through out all Manasseh, who also gathered behind him. He also sent messengers to Asher, Zebulun, and Naphtali; and they came up to meet them"

Gideon was willing to serve the Lord. Gideon knew the threat was great and the risk was high. He also knew in his heart that if he and the people of God were going to be victorious, then God would have to show up. So what does Gideon do? He blows the trumpet of war. This, my friend, was an act of faith. Gideon believed that God had called him to this moment. Gideon believed that God would show up with power.

You know God can show up in many ways, and in verse 34 God blesses Gideon with His Spirit. The Spirit of the Lord came upon Gideon. Even though Gideon had been through some testing and training his greatest asset was the Spirit of God. You know, all of the talents and abilities in the world are useless without the Holy Spirit's help.

Notice that the text says, "The Spirit of the Lord *came upon* Gideon". That phrase "came upon" in the Hebrew text means to wrap around or to put on like a garment. The phrase can also mean to arm or to wear. As we read this text we need to understand that the Spirit of the Lord empowered, anointed and surrounded Gideon's life. The Spirit of the Lord was upon this man that was willing to serve God. Today, when one of God's children decides to willfully serve Him, they too are blessed with the empowerment of the Holy Spirit. Instead of being surrounded by the Holy Spirit as in the Old Testament scriptures, a person today that is born again is indwelt with the Spirit of God.

Today in many of our pulpits the Holy Spirit is rarely taught and preached. If a person is going to be spirit led, then that same person must know what the Holy Spirit looks like. The word of God paints us a picture of the Holy Spirit. The Holy Spirit is not as mysterious and illusive as we would like to think. In fact, the gospel of John chapter 16 reveals much about the Holy Spirit. If you want to know how God can show up read and study these verses.

John 16:13-14 (NKJV) [13] *However, when He, the Spirit of truth, has come, He will guide you into all truth; for He will not speak on His own authority, but whatever He hears He will speak; and He will tell you things to come.* [14] *He will glorify Me, for He will take of what is Mine and declare it to you.*

The Spirit of the Lord came upon Gideon. In other words, God showed up. Friend, God will help you accomplish whatever He calls you to pursue.

Well, not only did God bless Gideon with His Spirit, God also blessed Gideon with some followers. When Gideon blew the trumpet God's people lined up for battle. In fact, they came from all around. God's people that had been oppressed by the enemy, Gods people that had been dominated by fear, Gods people that had been hiding in caves now have gathered behind their new leader Gideon.

Here we find a great truth. A group of people always need a leader. People don't always submit to leaders but at the end of the day they're usually glad that someone was leading the way. Gideon had heard God's call and had become the leader of God's people, and the people rallied behind him. I believe they began to realize that God's Spirit was with Gideon and that God really cared about their circumstances. The Israelites believed like the Apostle Paul, "What then shall we say to these things? If God *is* for us then who *can be* against us?" Romans 8:31, NKJV

There are many lessons to be learned from Gideon's example. For instance, when a person accepts God's role for their life and is willing to serve Him faithfully, they can be assured that God will not only show up but will help them become victorious. Another lesson that we can glean is the "No Lone Ranger" principle. Within the body of Christ there should be no lone rangers. God has called us to work together. In our text, Gideon blows the trumpet and God sends people from every direction. When we try to do it all ourselves we deprive others of serving. By the way, God has called all of His children to serve Him. Remember, the title of this section is "God calls us to serve".

Today, are you serving God? What has God called you to do? Are you serving the Lord through a local church? If so, continue to be faithful, keep serving the Lord and be open to other areas of service in the future. If you're not serving the

The Gideon in You

Lord, why? If you don't know why then turn the page, the next chapter maybe why you opened this book.

Chapter Fifteen

"Why do some people fail to serve God?"

If you notice I have broken my pattern in writing this book. At the beginning of each chapter I have provided a set of verses that reveal a progression that takes place in Judges chapter six. But here in this chapter we need to sit down and talk for just a moment. We need to ask some questions concerning why some people serve the Lord while others simply show up at church on Sunday. Let's begin with the positive. Here are some of the reasons I serve the Lord.

First, Jesus Christ died for me. Really, when you think about it we shouldn't have to list any other reason for serving Him. When someone willingly lays down their life so that another person can live, that's powerful. In fact, it's life changing. Because of His sacrifice and love for me, I can't help but serve Him.

Second, God has called me to serve Him. Serving God should not be optional for the Christian. In the great commission in Matthew 28:19-20 we are not only called but commanded to make disciples and teach others what Christ has taught us.

Third, I also serve God because He has given me spiritual gifts and talents by the power of the Holy Spirit. The very gifts and talents that people possess today were given to them by God for the purpose of serving Him not themselves.

The fourth reason I serve God is very simple but powerful. When I willingly serve Him, He is glorified. My service to Him will point others to God the Father and Jesus Christ His only begotten Son. The hope is that others will see good works in my life and glorify my Father in heaven.

Now there are many others reasons for serving the Lord, these are just a few. But the question of this chapter remains. Why do some people fail to serve God?

Rejection

First, some people reject God altogether. They reject His offer of salvation, they reject God's only begotten Son Jesus Christ, and they reject the sacrifice that was made on their behalf. They simply say to God, "I don't need you and I see no need of serving you". Some people feel like they can handle life on their own and see no need in including God in their lives. So they tragically reject God, completely. And if you study the bible you find that God gives every person the right to reject Him. He does not force a person to accept His love, His grace and His mercy. That is the kind of God that we have the opportunity to serve. However, in spite of His great love for mankind, some people still refuse to serve God because they reject him altogether.

Lack Of Trust

The second reason I believe people fail to serve the Lord is a lack of trust. It's a trust issue. If a person is going to serve the Lord according to His will, then they are going to have to trust Him completely. They are going to have to take God at His Word and trust Him. They are going to have to trust God for the strength, power and ability to accomplish His purpose for their life.

As I am privileged to pastor one of God's churches I have found that most people, including Christians, want to be in charge of their own life. In fact, most people feel like they know what's best for their life. The truth? We can barely tie our shoes on our own. We really need God's help. In order for God to be able to help us, we are going to have to trust Him with the unknown, that's where walking by faith comes in to play. To walk by faith a person must trust God. It cannot be optional. We must trust God if we are going to serve Him.

We must trust His sovereignty and providence if we are going to walk with Him. Sovereignty speaks of Gods power and His ability to exercise His own authority. Providence speaks of Gods power to bring to pass that which He has promised. With that said, I can't think of anyone else we should trust with our lives, can you?

My personal belief is that many of Gods children have not paid attention to God's sovereignty and providence as they have turned the pages of scripture. The evidence of our need to trust Him with our lives is impressive. The evidence of our need to serve Him is undeniable. But again, some people have trouble trusting anyone much less someone that they have never physically seen.

Good Old Fashioned Fear

The third reason I believe people fail to serve the Lord is fear. They are simply afraid. Now, I do want to paint the proper biblical picture for you. Serving the Lord is most often difficult and risky. If someone tells you otherwise, check the scriptures and listen to Moses, Elijah and Daniel. Their testimonies will tell you that serving the Lord can be frightening at times. The things that God calls us to do are not always popular with the world and the enemies of God.

Some people have heard horror stories of Christians serving God and losing their lives for the cause of Christ. Others have heard testimonies of cruel treatment or persecution that came as a result of serving the Lord. Still others have tried to witness to a lost friend or loved one only to be rejected. Guess what? There is real fear and pain in all of the above. Sadly, some count the cost and decide that they are going to sit in the pew and let someone else get the job done. The result? That person lets fear paralyze them and they fail to serve God.

While Moses, Elijah and Daniel faced real fears they also rose to the occasion and met the challenge with Gods help. The apostle Paul in the New Testament faced horrible circumstances but chose to crucify his fears daily in order to serve Christ. Paul knew that his faith would cast aside his fears.

Listen, when a person decides to willfully serve the Lord persecution will come, its part of the identity we have in Jesus Christ. Jesus in John 15:20 said, "Remember the word that I said to you, 'A servant is not greater than his master.' If they persecuted Me, they will also persecute you. If they kept My word, they will keep yours also."

If we follow and serve the Lord we will be persecuted by man. We can either accept what Jesus has told us or we can shrink back in fear and fail to serve Him. If we allow fear to paralyze us to the point that we fail to serve the Lord, then we are going to have to give an account to God when we stand before Him. If you are afraid to serve the Lord, read your bible, believe what God's word says, and fear God more than man.

Wrong Perception

Fourth, some people fail to serve the Lord because they have the wrong perspective. They feel unworthy or unable to serve the Lord. In false humility, many Christians will say they feel so unworthy to serve the Lord, or they feel that they don't have much to offer God.

The truth is this, without the Holy Spirit of God indwelling us, empowering us, directing us and gifting us, we could not serve the Lord for one minute, period. We need the Holy Spirit's help. If a person has been born again, then they have the presence of God living within them. The Holy Spirit was given to those that believe so that they might be sanctified. To be sanctified means "to be set apart". Through the power of the Holy Spirit followers of Christ are able to serve the Lord because He has made them worthy and able to serve.

So, the Christian that fails to serve God on the grounds of their unworthiness or their inability is really slapping the Holy Spirit in the face. Their perception is wrong. If this is you I want to challenge you to study the bible and believe what God's word says about you. The scriptures will tell you "who you are and what you can do" in Christ. Note that I said, "in Christ". In John 15:5 Jesus says, **"I am the vine, you *are* the branches. He who abides in Me, and I in him, bears much fruit; for without Me you can do nothing."**

With that said, what kind of perception do you have? Do you perceive that God can and will work through you for His glory? Do you have a biblical perspective concerning who you are in Christ?

Now these are just some of the reasons people fail to serve the Lord. In fact, my wife and I were discussing this topic and she advised me to cut it short that I could write many chapters on this subject. As always, my wife is right.

The bottom line is this, everyone that does not know Jesus Christ personally as Lord and Savior needs to be reconciled to God through His sacrifice on the cross. If that is you, then I compel you to consider giving your heart to Christ, turn away from sin and turn toward the Savior. Ask God to forgive you of your sins, ask God to save you and become the Lord of your life. That is your first step to serving Him.

If you have already become a child of God by placing your trust in Jesus Christ, then your next step is to serve Him. Lay aside all fear and reservations and serve Him. Get involved in a local bible believing church, talk to the pastor and he will guide you as you walk with the Lord. And when the fear of serving God rises up, cast it aside and walk by faith. The next thing you know the "Gideon In You" will rise to the occasion and God will begin to grow your faith and do great things through your life.

Section Five

"God Grows Our Faith"

Chapter Sixteen
"Victory Without Faith Is Impossible"

Hebrews 11:6, NKJV

"But without faith it is *impossible to please* Him, *for he who comes to God must believe that He is, and* that *He is a rewarder of those who diligently seek Him."*

Faith is taking God at His word. Which means at times we are called to believe the unbelievable. Hebrews 11:1 says, *"Now faith is the substance of things hoped for, the evidence of things not seen."* When you consider that verse you come away with an understanding that God expects us to hope for things that we cannot visually see. That's why victory without faith is impossible. A person cannot have victory over sin, death and the grave unless they put their faith in Jesus Christ. Again, eternal life, this incredible victory is impossible to obtain unless a person has faith.

We also need to live by faith in order to walk with God. The author of the New Testament book of Hebrews writes about heroes of the faith in chapter eleven. He admits that time would not permit him to give an account of all of the victories that were won by faith. Listen to what the author of Hebrews writes in chapter eleven.

> [32] "And what more shall I say? For the time would fail me to tell of Gideon and Barak and Samson and Jephthah, also of David and Samuel and the prophets: [33] who through faith subdued kingdoms, worked righteousness, obtained promises, stopped the mouths of lions, [34] quenched the violence of fire, escaped the edge of the sword, out of weakness were made strong, became valiant in battle, turned to flight the armies of the aliens. [35] Women received their dead raised to life again. And others were tortured, not accepting deliverance, that they might obtain a better resurrection. [36] Still others had trial of mockings and scourgings, yes, and of chains and imprisonment. [37] They were stoned, they were sawn in two, were tempted, were slain with the sword. They wandered about in sheepskins and goatskins, being destitute, afflicted, tormented-- [38] of whom the world was not worthy. They wandered in deserts and mountains, in dens and caves of the earth. [39] And all these, having obtained a good testimony through faith, did not receive the promise," Hebrews 11:32-39, NKJV

Talking about real faith, battles were fought, victories were won and the Lord glorified all because God's people demonstrated real faith, faith that pleased God. Through faith great goals were accomplished, great suffering was endured and great testimonies were established.

Guess what? If we, God's people, are going to accomplish anything noteworthy it's going to have to be done by faith and through faith. Our faith in God must be the deciding factor in all that we set out to achieve for the kingdom. In fact the New Testament is crystal clear concerning this topic of faith.

Romans 1:17 says, we are to live by faith, **"For in it the righteousness of God is revealed from faith to faith; as it is written, "The just shall live by faith.""**

Romans 4:12 says, we are to walk by faith, **"and the father of circumcision to those who not only are of the circumcision, but who also walk in the steps of the faith which our father Abraham had while still uncircumcised."**

Matthew 21:22 says, we are to pray by faith, **"And whatever things you ask in prayer, believing, you will receive."**

We are also to resist the devil by faith, overcome the world by faith and we are suppose to die in the faith. Taking into consideration all that we have heard, God wants you and I to be completely sold out to Him. He longs for us to believe in Him, to trust Him whole heartedly. He calls us to believe Him for all that He has promised. His word directs us to believe in Him for the victory.

What does all of this mean for young Gideon? He too would have to trust God for the victory. With the Midianites and the Amalekites breathing down his neck, Gideon was going to have to trust God with his life and the nation Israel. Without faith the victory would be impossible.

Remember, Gideon had been called by God to lead God's people into battle against His enemies. Gideon has now stepped into the role of leader, deliverer, and military commander. And while Gideon has some faith, his faith still needs to grow.

As a follower of Christ our faith needs to continually grow. The apostle Peter at the close of his second epistle admonishes us to keep growing in the Lord.

> *"but grow in the grace and knowledge of our Lord and Savior Jesus Christ. To Him be the glory both now and forever. Amen."* 2 Peter 3:18, NKJV

The apostle Peter knew that faith was needed in order for a person to live the victorious Christian life. If you and I are going to allow the "Gideon in us" to rise to the surface, faith is going to have to play an important role. Remember, without faith it is impossible to please God. As you read the bible you can't help but notice that faith and victory go hand in hand. Wherever you find a great victory, somebody nearby had some faith. Whenever great things for God were accomplished, faith was always present.

As we have read about Gideon, we've found that Gideon's faith still needed to grow. How about your faith? Does your faith need to grow? Are you trusting God more than you did one year ago? Have you been trusting God with the unseen future that lies ahead? Are you allowing your faith to grow by serving God faithfully?

As you turn the page you will find that even while walking by faith, doubts can still arise from time to time. But when they do, we need to come to God and ask Him by faith to help grow our faith in Him. If you will choose to operate this way, you will be able to smell the victory that is soon to come.

Chapter Seventeen

"Asking By Faith"

Judges 6:36-38, NKJV

[36] So Gideon said to God, "If You will save Israel by my hand as You have said-- [37] look, I shall put a fleece of wool on the threshing floor; if there is dew on the fleece only, and it is dry on all the ground, then I shall know that You will save Israel by my hand, as You have said." [38] And it was so. When he rose early the next morning and squeezed the fleece together, he wrung the dew out of the fleece, a bowlful of water.

Can you believe that? Gideon, after all that he had seen and heard, is still asking God to prove Himself. Gideon says, "God, if this is really what you want me to do, then give me a sign". Have you ever been in that kind of shape before? A time when God had revealed so much to you, but you still kept asking Him for more. Unfortunately, I think this is common ground for most people.

The Gideon in You

Today, we live within a culture that demands proof, a culture that is driven by sight and not by faith, a world that doesn't trust anyone, much less a God whom they have never physically seen. Even when God does the inexplicable and makes the impossible possible, we still want more proof. Gideon could have lived today without having to change his approach.

In our text we find Gideon asking for a sign. Did you notice that Gideon gets really specific? The request would require the use of a fleece (which is freshly sheared wool), the dirt on the ground, the dew that falls from the sky overnight, and the hand of God. Gideons role in all of this? He was to place the fleece on the ground, and believe God for the miracle. The next morning if the dew was only on the fleece, while the ground remained dry, then God was confirming His call upon Gideon's life to lead His people into battle.

Can you imagine the anticipation that Gideon felt overnight? Remember when you were a kid trying to fall asleep on Christmas Eve? You couldn't wait to get up the next morning to see all of the presents under the tree. And when morning finally came you couldn't get down the hall and into the living room fast enough. Your heart was beating with excitement. I imagine Gideon went to sleep that night with great anticipation. Perhaps, thinking to himself, "will God really grant me this sign?".

Well, verse 38 says "and it was so". Like Christmas day, Gideon rose early the next morning and went outside to check his fleece. Sure enough, God had granted his request. The fleece was soaked and the ground was dry. God had made the impossible, possible. Now, you would think that God had proven Himself enough. Did you notice that Gideon picked up the fleece and wrung the dew out into a bowl? The result, his cup runs over, or in Gideon's case his bowl.

Isn't that just like God to exceed our expectations? God never fails to amaze me. When He blesses us, he blesses us with abundance. Gideon wakes up and finds a miracle, the very miracle that he asked God to grant. So, end of story, Gideon's faith had finally grown enough, right? Wrong. Gideon wanted even more proof. What did he do? He did the unthinkable. He asked God for another sign.

Judges 6:39-40, NKJV
" Then Gideon said to God, "Do not be angry with me, but let me speak just once more: Let me test, I pray, just once more with the fleece; let it now be dry only on the fleece, but on all the ground let there be dew." ⁴⁰ And God did so that night. It was dry on the fleece only, but there was dew on all the ground."

Gideon reminds me of the Old Testament patriarch Abraham. When Abraham was pleading for God to save his nephew Lot and his family, he kept asking God to grant his request and in Genesis 18:30 Abraham says, *"let not the Lord be angry"*. Here we find Gideon wants to ask the Lord to give him another sign, but at the same time he doesn't want God to be angry.

Did you notice, once again Gideon gets really specific? The same elements were involved, the fleece, the ground, the dew and the hand of God. But there was a change in the order of things. Gideon asks God to reverse the miracle. In fact, he asks God to make the fleece dry and allow the dew to only fall on the ground.

What was Gideon thinking? Maybe Gideon was thinking that the first sign could happen naturally. I suppose Gideon could have reasoned away God's miracle. If this was Gideon's approach he would really be at home in the world today. We are living in a day in which science tries to reason away every existence of God. Miracles of God are explained away and people that actually believe the bible are considered naïve. Again, the world wants proof of God's existence. One of the purposes of this book is to prove to you that the only real proof of God's existence is <u>your changed life</u>. When we as individuals allow God to work in and through our lives, we prove to a lost and dieing world that Jesus Christ is not only alive but on His throne. So, if the world in which you live wants proof of God, allow God to continually change your life. Allow the "Gideon in you" to point others to Christ.

We could speculate all day long as to why Gideon would ask God for another sign. I simply believe Gideon was looking for assurance. In the next chapter we will talk about motives and how they relate to asking God for signs. For now, let's follow the story a little further. Once again we find in verse 40 the assurance Gideon was looking for, *"And God did so that night. It was dry on the fleece only, but there was dew on all the ground."*

God once again shows great grace and mercy to Gideon. Not only that, He establishes and grows Gideon's faith. By the way, Gideon was not asking God to grant him signs from a lack of faith. Gideon had faith. But if Gideon was going to lead God's people to victory then his faith was going to have to increase. This testing and these trials that Gideon faced may have seemed trivial, but they were needed. And while Gideon was in need of more faith, at the same time he had enough faith to come boldly to God's throne and ask God for the two signs. If you really examine the last couple of days in Gideon's life, he had come accustomed to seeing some miracles.

- The Angel of the Lord appears and speaks to him on a few occasions.
- The meat and the broth he prepared for the angel was consumed by fire from heaven.

- Gideon tore down the altar of Baal and lived to tell about it.
- Gideon now has the Holy Spirit upon his life.
- He blows the trumpet of war and after years of oppression and defeat God's people respond and are ready to fight for their land.

When you consider all that Gideon had witnessed, I believe, in humility, Gideon wanted to see more. So what does Gideon do? He asks by faith.

Coming boldly to God's throne, as a child of God, and asking Him for the things we need is absolutely appropriate and an essential part of the Christian life. Jesus time and time again instructed his followers to ask their Heavenly Father for the things they needed.

Matthew 7:7-11, NKJV
"Ask, and it will be given to you; seek, and you will find; knock, and it will be opened to you. [8] For everyone who asks receives, and he who seeks finds, and to him who knocks it will be opened. [9] Or what man is there among you who, if his son asks for bread, will give him a stone? [10] Or if he asks for a fish, will he give him a serpent? [11] If you then, being evil, know how to give good gifts to your children, how much more will your Father who is in heaven give good things to those who ask Him!"

Do you think Jesus wants us to ask Him for the things that we need? And if the answer is yes, and it is, shouldn't we believe that God not only hears us but will help us with those same needs? Jesus once again in Matthew chapter twenty one talks about asking in the appropriate way, by faith.

The Gideon in You

> *Matthew 21:22, NKJV*
> *"And whatever things you ask in prayer, believing, you will receive."*

Notice, Jesus says when we ask by faith we will receive. Gideon asked for the two signs, but in reality he was asking for assurance. Gideon was asking by faith, believing to receive. Have you discovered that this book, "The Gideon In You", is really about faith? Lets get really specific, your faith. Do you believe God? Do you believe that God wants to continually transform your life into the life of a servant? Do you believe that God not only wants to do great things in your life, but can do great things through your life? Guess what? The ball is in your court. It's up to you. Will you trust God with your life? Gideon was facing this same question. Turn the page and let's check out Gideon's motives and at the same time take inventory of our own.

Chapter Eighteen

"God Blesses the Right Motives"

What kind of motives do you have? Do you have the right motives or wrong motives? Let's get real. Why do you do what you do?

As we look at the life of Gideon we find him asking God for some signs. We need to understand that we don't need to go through this life continually asking God for signs. I do believe there are times when it is appropriate. And by the way, asking God for a sign is not necessarily a dangerous thing. That is, if you have the right motive. When a person with ill motives asks God for a sign, then it becomes trouble.

In Jesus' day, the ill-motivated religious leaders asked Jesus for a sign. In fact, they sought to trap Jesus in His words and they tried to discredit Jesus' miracles. Their motives were wrong. Their intent was to have Jesus killed. Jesus in response to their request for a sign told them that the only sign their wicked generation would receive was the sign of Jonah. Jesus, of course, was eluding to His own death, burial and resurrection. And even though these men were religious leaders, they still didn't understand Jesus' words. In short, their motives were less than good.

Jesus would also encounter another man asking Him for a sign, King Herod. King Herod wanted Jesus to perform some kind of miracle before his very eyes. King Herod was a curiosity seeker with bad motives. Herod wanted to be entertained. This is a good place for a Jesus infomercial. Jesus wears many hats. He is King of Kings, Lord of Lords, Savior, Redeemer, the Lamb of God, the Great I AM, and the list goes on for eternity. However, Jesus is not an entertainer. He does not do parlor tricks to amuse or entertain. Jesus is not some genie in a bottle granting wishes. He is the Lord. King Herod and his bad motives did not receive a sign from Jesus, and neither will you and I if our motives are selfish, fleshly and sinful.

Gideon, however, asks for these signs in humility. What was his motive? Gideon wanted to make sure that he didn't hurt God's people. Gideon wanted to make sure that he was doing the will of God. He didn't want to risk the lives of Gods' people unless God was calling the nation into battle.

When God called me into the gospel ministry, I asked God for some signs. What was my motive? I didn't want to hurt people. In fact, I wanted to help people. Going against Gods plan will hurt people every time. I somehow understood this great fact. On top of that I didn't want to lay down a twelve year career unless God was truly calling me. I was concerned with hurting my family and others if I was wrong. So what did I do? I asked God for some signs. What did God do? He blessed me time and time again.

Once instance I remember like it was yesterday. It was in the spring of 2000. God had given me the opportunity to supply preach at Rocky Valley Baptist Church in Lebanon, Tn. I had only preached about a dozen sermons so I was still very wet behind the ears. I preached a sermon entitled "Escape Or Fulfillment". The sermon talked about accepting the will of God and pursuing it, or hearing from God and attempting to escape. There was a point about midway in the message where the Holy Spirit whispered into my heart that this was going to be my pulpit. My prayer was "Lord, if this is your will I will come here." I went on to supply at Rocky Valley for nine more weeks. My family and I knew we were at our new church home, the church knew it as well. The pastor search committee, however, had not approached me. My nine weeks were coming to a close on Easter Sunday and still there was no official word. What did I do? By faith, I asked God for a sign. I asked God to have the three men on the pastor search committee to say something official to me that day. Not the chairman, but all three individually. I got specific.

Easter morning was ushered in with a long time tradition at Rocky Valley, a sunrise service. It was my first and it was awesome. After our small group visited the crosses up on the hill, we made our way back to the old fellowship hall in the basement. It was there at the bottom of the stairwell that the first committee member said something. It was Larry. Larry said, "give us a couple of weeks and we will give you a call, we believe you are our pastor." I was thrilled. Was I shocked? Not really. I think I just simply believed the Holy Spirit's testimony during that first sermon. After Larry walked away I said, "Lord, that's one."

Later that morning everyone attended Sunday School. Between Sunday School and worship Charles stopped me in the aisle and said, "we'll talk to you in a couple of weeks, we are going to meet with the stewardship committee in a few days." As Charles walked away, I said, "That's two Lord."

After the evening worship service the church had a fellowship meal for me and my family. People were expressing their appreciation and love for us, some were even crying at the thought of us leaving. Our nine weeks together had been special. As this Easter day continued I was still looking for the third man on the committee to say something. As we were saying our good-byes Jim gave me a hug. Jim said, "Buddy, we'll talk to you soon." On the inside I said, "Lord, that's three."

If man had guided those circumstances only one from the committee would have spoken to me, the chairman. Instead, just as I asked, all three made a comment. God had given me my sign.

What was God doing in this process? God was confirming, establishing and growing my faith. The intent of this chapter is not to send you out asking God for all kinds of signs. The intent is to make you aware of Gods' desire to grow your faith. When your motives are right, when you are seeking to accomplish His will, when you are continually seeking His hand upon your life, He blesses. God blesses the right motives.

Gideon had the right motives. His heart was in the right place. He didn't want to cause pain. Instead he wanted Gods' people to be blessed. Gideon, with all of his right motives, asked God for many signs, and God blessed him tremendously.

What about you? What about your motives? Why do you do what you do? When you come to God asking, seeking and knocking, why and how do you come? Do you come in humility? Do you come by faith? To live the victorious Christian life we must be humble and we must be full of faith. Is God growing your faith?

Have you ever considered the fact that healthy things grow? And when healthy things grow they usually change. In fact, for a tree to grow it must change. Wouldn't it be ridiculous for us to want a tree to grow and at the same time ask it to stay the same?

My oldest daughter has recently become a teen-ager. Needless to say, things are changing at my house. Why are they changing? Well, my family is growing up. My three girls are getting older. As they grow, they change. It would be crazy for me to expect my girls to grow up and not change. Growth and change go hand in hand.

Churches often times want to grow, but they seldom want to change. The more the church grows, the more some people try to keep everything the same. Again, healthy things grow. And things that grow always change.

Would you agree, like Gideon, our faith needs to grow? If our faith needs to grow, then that means that we also need to change. Gods' desire is to grow our faith and help us become more and more like His Son Jesus Christ. The Apostle Paul in Romans 8:29 helps us understand this great truth, **"For whom He foreknew, He also predestined** to be *conformed to the image of His Son, that He might be the firstborn among many brethren." Romans 8:29 (NKJV)*

Before moving on to the next chapter, take inventory of your motives. Ask yourself some tough questions. Spend some time in prayer. And last, but certainly not least, make a decision to allow God to grow your faith and purify your motives. If you follow this counsel, you will begin to discover "The Gideon In You."

Section Six

"Gods' Way Is The Only Way"

Chapter Nineteen

"Reduction Is Necessary For Victory"

As a father of three girls I have discovered that as we drive in our family mini-van, my children are always concerned with "where" we are going. As we take family vacations they pester me with the common question "are we there yet?". At the very heart of all of their comments and questions is the hope that we, as a family, are making some progress.

In reading through the previous chapters you might be asking the same kind of questions. Where have we been? Where are we going? What have we learned? Let's recap for just a minute and see the progression of Judges Chapter six.

Here is what we see as we look back over the road we have traveled. We will glance back by sections.

1. **God calls us to salvation**. God not only knows that we are in need of salvation. He also provides that same salvation. But thanks to God, He doesn't stop with providing His Son Jesus Christ as our savior, He also calls us to salvation. He draws us by the power of the Holy Spirit and convicts us of sin, righteousness and judgment.

2. **God blesses us when we give.** When we sacrifice our lives, God takes notice and blesses us. When we freely give an offering to God, He is pleased. When we take the time to be in His presence through worship, He never disappoints us.
3. **God tests those He calls.** As God calls us to salvation and then begins to work on our lives, He tests our hearts. When God calls you and I to do great things, He will normally perform a spiritual EKG on our hearts. He tests those He calls in order to determine if our hearts are truly bent toward Him.
4. **God calls us to serve.** Being a follower of Jesus Christ and serving God goes hand in hand. God calls us to salvation so that we can be delivered from the power of sin, death and the grave. God calls us to salvation so that we can be with Him for all of eternity. But now God has also called us to salvation so that we can serve Him. We are to be witnesses for Him. God calls us to serve.
5. **God grows our faith.** While reading through the previous four sections we discover that in order to walk with God and serve Him, we must have faith. And while having faith is a good thing, that same faith needs to grow. For God to use us for His glory, for God to give us more responsibility in the kingdom, our faith must grow. Therefore, God grows our faith.

Considering our recap we now come to this section entitled "Gods' way is the only way." We cannot serve God and bring glory to God if we are determined to do it our way. For instance, Gods' will is accomplished….

Not in our strength, but Gods'…
Not by our power, but Gods'…

Not with our own reasoning, but by faith...
Not with our flesh, but by the Spirit...
Not according to tradition, but according to Gods' word...

The bottom line is this, when it comes to accomplishing Gods' will, "Gods' way is the only way." As individual Christians and as individual churches we must operate according to Gods' word if we are going to impact our world for Jesus Christ.

With the title of this section in mind, we return to Gideon and find him setting himself up for battle. Gideon has a good number of soldiers ready to battle the Midianites, thirty-two thousand. All along, Gideon believed that God would keep His promise. By the way, what is this promise? God promised Gideon that He, God, would give the Israelites victory over the enemy.

When I consider all of the great truths that a person can learn from the bible, the truth of Gods' faithfulness is at the top of the list. God is faithful. In other words, God always keeps His word. God can always be trusted. When He makes a promise, you can take it to the bank. He means what He says, and says what He means.

In Judges Chapter seven this promise of God is going to come true. But in the process of fulfilling His promise, God says to Gideon "you've got too many soldiers". As we read chapter seven we find that in order for God to get the glory for this victory, a great reduction was needed.

Judges 7:1-3 (NKJV)
[1]Then Jerubbaal (that is, Gideon) and all the people who were with him rose early and encamped beside the well of Harod, so that the camp of the Midianites was on the north side of them by the hill of Moreh in the valley. [2] And the Lord said to Gideon, "The people who are with you are too many for Me to give the

Midianites into their hands, lest Israel claim glory for itself against Me, saying, 'My own hand has saved me.' ³ Now therefore, proclaim in the hearing of the people, saying, 'Whoever is fearful and afraid, let him turn and depart at once from Mount Gilead.' " And twenty-two thousand of the people returned, and ten thousand remained.

God knows exactly "who we are", He knows our motives, and He knows what makes us tick. God knows us from the inside – out. The bible in Jeremiah 1:5 proclaims this great truth concerning God, *"Before I formed you in the womb I knew you; Before you were born I sanctified you; I ordained you a prophet to the nations."* God knows all about us. Here in chapter seven God says to Gideon, *"the people who are with you are too many for me."* God knew that if Gideon were to defeat the enemy with 32,000 men that Gideon would think that they themselves brought the victory instead of God.

Can you imagine what was going through the mind of Gideon? Gideon was probably thinking just how blessed he was to have 32,000 willing men. In fact, even with this large number Gods' people were going to be grossly out-numbered by the Midianites. This must have been a severe blow to Gideon's morale.

But now, let's not miss this all important lesson from the word of God. God knows that "man" likes to receive recognition. Lets face it, we like getting some of the credit, we like a pat on the back every now and then. Am I right? Mankind likes to think that "he" has done something.

When I think of the ill motives of "man" I look back into Genesis and remember the tower of Babel (Genesis 11). If you remember, the whole earth had only one language and one purpose in mind. Mankind wanted to prove that it could sustain itself. Take a moment and read this passage from

Genesis chapter eleven and see if it resembles the "world system" of today.

> *Genesis 11:3-4 (NKJV)*
> *³ Then they said to one another, "Come, let us make bricks and bake them thoroughly." They had brick for stone, and they had asphalt for mortar. ⁴ And they said, "Come, let us build ourselves a city, and a tower whose top is in the heavens; let us make a name for ourselves, lest we be scattered abroad over the face of the whole earth."*

Did you hear what the people were saying? They wanted to "make a name for themselves". If we were to read further we find that God did not tolerate that type of behavior. In fact He scatters the people by confusing their languages. Due to communication barriers the people couldn't make a name for themselves by building this tower.

The God of heaven, the God of the bible, the one true living God, is a jealous God. He is the only one deserving of "true glory". He seeks to be recognized, honored and worshipped. In the day of Babel, there was no room for God to be second. In Gideon's day there was no room for God to be second. And guess what? Today, God still wants to be first. He still wants to be recognized, honored and worshipped. He wants the credit, He wants the glory.

When you think about all that God has done, doesn't He deserve all the credit? That's what He is pointing out to Gideon in Judges chapter seven. If 32,000 men were to go into battle and win, they could take credit for the victory. God desperately wanted His people to understand that Gods' way to victory was the only way. So, He reduces the troops down by 2/3 and leaves Gideon with 10,000 men. But how did God do it?

God says to Gideon, "proclaim to the people", "whoever is fearful and afraid go home." And they did, 22,000 men decide to return to their homes. Now remember, 32,000 men showed up when Gideon blew his trumpet for war in chapter six, but when the chips were down and the battle was in front of them, 22,000 decided to bail out and go home.

They were afraid. Maybe they couldn't stomach the perils of battle, or maybe it was simply a lack of commitment. However you slice it, 2/3 of Gideon's army chose to go home. A great reduction in troops took place.

Today, God knows the intent of the human heart. He knows who is committed to His cause. God knows if you and I are truly committed to His mission.
- God knows who is willing to do the difficult.
- God knows who is willing to battle spiritually.
- God knows who will be submissive to His way of doing things.
- God knows who cares for the things of God.
- God knows who is willing to stand in the face of adversity.

In Gideon's case 22,000 men chose…
Not to get involved in the fight….
Not to stand in faith, but to flee in fear…
To watch from the sidelines as their freedom and their land was fought over…

Today, if the body of Christ is going to impact the future population of hell, then we are going to have to be willing to stand in the faith and fight for people's souls. If we are going to be the servants of God that He has called us to be then we are going to have to "fall in" and be willing to do the difficult.

We need to also understand that God can do much with little. In this story of Gideon we find that God can win victories with a "fully committed" minority. If you're thinking that God can't accomplish His will without you, you are wrong. In fact, He can do it all by Himself if He so desires. But you know what? He desires to give us the privilege of partnering with Him on this mission of saving mankind.

    Gideon watched 22,000 troops go home, fearful and afraid, refusing to take part in Gods' plan. I know, you have a question, wasn't God wanting to reduce the number of troops? Yes. In Gods' sovereignty, He knew the hearts of thousands of men that didn't really want to fight for their freedom and their land. So, He sent them home. God sent home 22,000 men, but now that's the first reduction. Let's read a little further and witness God whittle down Gideon's army like a piece of cedar.

> *Judges 7:4-6 (NKJV)*
> *⁴ But the Lord said to Gideon, "The people* are *still too many; bring them down to the water, and I will test them for you there. Then it will be,* that *of whom I say to you, 'This one shall go with you,' the same shall go with you; and of whomever I say to you, 'This one shall not go with you,' the same shall not go." ⁵ So he brought the people down to the water. And the Lord said to Gideon, "Everyone who laps from the water with his tongue, as a dog laps, you shall set apart by himself; likewise everyone who gets down on his knees to drink." ⁶ And the number of those who lapped,* putting *their hand to their mouth, was three hundred men; but all the rest of the people got down on their knees to drink water.*

    Here we find God, once again, reducing the number of troops. Once again, if Gideon were to win the battle with 10,000 men, he might pat himself on the back instead of God. So, God gives Gideon some instructions. God has Gideon bring the men down to the river for a test. Remember, God tests those He calls. God tests them with a drink of water. In fact, God was interested in the method in which these men took their drink. As we read in verses 5-6 we find that the majority of the men drank the water on their knees. They were on their knees with their faces in the water. You might be asking, "What's the problem?" The problem lies within their posture. A soldier that prostrates himself in such a way while drinking water, is more concerned with meeting his own need rather than being mindful of an approaching enemy. The others however, bent down and lapped their water with their hands. Here we see this second reduction in troops, 9,700 men are sent home. Gideon is now left with 300 troops, roughly 1% of the 32,000 men that heard the first trumpet call. Gideon is about to learn that "Gods way to victory is the only way to victory".

Sometimes, God has to reduce you and I down to nothing in order to show us that He is everything that we need. When we try to pursue our dreams, our plans, our own direction, God has to sometimes intervene and prove to us that He alone is our sufficiency. Reduction in our lives is sometimes necessary.

When I think about victory over sin, death and the grave, I can't help but think about Gods' way of victory is the only way. The religious leaders of Jesus' day were looking for a Messiah that would bring them a victory over the Roman Empire. That was their idea of victory. Jesus, however, came for so much more. He came to give mankind victory over sin, death and the grave. In fact, He came to fight a battle that we could not win, to bring a victory that we ourselves could not obtain on our own.

In considering Gods' call to salvation, He invites us to have this victory over sin. But this victory is only possible through Gods' way, not our own. This world thinks it can produce a victory over sin, death and the grave some other way. The world is fatally wrong.

In the Gospel of John, Thomas, one of the disciples was concerned about having victory over the grave. Thomas was troubled over "how he would know the way to victory". *Jesus said to him, "I am the way, the truth, and the life. No one comes to the Father except through Me.* **John 14:6 (NKJV)**

Once again, we find that Gods' way is the only way to victory. Gideon and Thomas had to discover this great truth, along with many others we read about in scripture. Let me ask you a question. Have you discovered this great truth? Have you come to God for salvation, only to discover that victory over sin is accomplished His way, and His way alone? Have you put your faith and trust in Jesus Christ, the way, the truth and life?

While the world cries that there is another way…..Jesus says, "no one comes to the Father except through Me." The real question is this, who are you going to believe? The world and its attempt to work for salvation and make a name for itself….. or, are you going to believe the Word of God?

Gideon learned that Gods' way of victory is the only way. As you turn the page you will find that God has a great resolve. He promises Gideon that victory is on the way.

Chapter Twenty

"God Keeps His Promises"

Judges 7:7-14, NKJV

7 Then the Lord said to Gideon, "By the three hundred men who lapped I will save you, and deliver the Midianites into your hand. Let all the other *people go, every man to his place.*" **8** So the people took provisions and their trumpets in their hands. And he sent away all the rest of *Israel, every man to his tent, and* retained those three hundred men. Now the camp of Midian was below him in the valley. **9** It happened on the same night that the Lord said to him, "Arise, go down against the camp, for I have delivered it into your hand. **10** But if you are afraid to go down, go down to the camp with Purah your servant, **11** and you shall hear what they say; and afterward your hands shall be strengthened to go down against the camp." Then he went down with Purah his servant to the outpost of the armed men who were *in the camp.* **12** Now the Midianites and Amalekites, all the people of the East, were lying in the valley as numerous as locusts; and their camels were *without number, as the sand by the seashore in multitude.* **13** And when Gideon had come, there was a man telling a dream *to his companion. He said, "I have had a dream: To my surprise, a loaf of barley bread tumbled into the camp of Midian; it came to a tent and struck it so that it fell and overturned, and the tent collapsed." ¹⁴ Then his companion answered and said, "This is nothing else but the sword of Gideon the son of Joash, a man of Israel! Into his hand God has delivered Midian and the whole camp."*

When you read the bible, you can't help but walk away from it believing that God is a promise keeper. He is not just a promise maker. In fact, anyone can make a promise, whether they are ordinary or extraordinary. Making a promise is like starting something new. The real test of character and faith is when you get to witness someone complete a project or fulfill their promise.

Keeping a promise isn't the easiest thing in the world to do, is it? My ten year old daughter quickly reminds me when I fail to keep a promise. As parents there are times when we make bad promises to our children that we know we won't keep. Instead of disciplining our children or simply telling them no for a change, we come up with a shallow promise that we never intend to keep. Employers in the work place promise employees advancement, extra time off, pay raises and the list goes on to infinity. Most of the time those promises are not kept. We as fallen human beings are good at making a promise while keeping a promise is one of our greatest weaknesses. God has a different testimony. God keeps His promises. God is faithful. God has resolved to keep His word.

In our text we find that God once again tells Gideon that "by the three hundred men who lapped the water I will save you." There it is again, a promise, a promise from God that He intends to keep, a promise that does not hinge on thousands of soldiers being successful. God's promise to Gideon and to the nation Israel hinges only on His character and power. In fact, God's promise hinges on God's ability to keep His word.

So, how did the three hundred respond to this promise? As we see in verse eight they began to prepare for the battle. They took provisions and trumpets into their hands while the rest of Israel went back home to their tents. Thousands were going home to be comfortable, while these three hundred men were preparing to risk their lives.

In the meantime God is speaking to Gideon about His strategy. Let's remember, God Himself is speaking to Gideon, not an angel, Jehovah God. As the nation of Israel is perched on top of a ridge, God tells Gideon to go down into the valley where the Midianites are sleeping. And in verse ten we hear our sovereign God tell Gideon that "if he is afraid he is to take his servant Purah with him". Friend, God knows that Gideon is afraid. He knows when you are afraid. At the same time He offers us grace for those moments. For Gideon, God offers him an option of taking his servant with him, and Gideon gladly accepts.

But now, what could God be up to? God has already whittled down the army from thousands to three hundred, now He is sending Gideon and Purah into this valley where the enemy is asleep. Why? Why would God send these two men into the enemy's camp alone? How could Gideon profit from this risk? What could he gain? The answer to all of these questions is simple, confidence in God.

Gideon's faith had been tested by God a hand full of times, while Gideon Himself tested God's faithfulness a few times of his own. God not only knew this but He also knew that Gideon's faith needed to be even stronger. So, what does God do? He boosts the confidence of Gideon. Gideon's faith in God that had grown so much in such a short time got an even greater boost.

When Gideon and Purah get to the Midianite camp they look to the ground and see soldiers and camels everywhere. The comedian in me can't help but think about the obvious smell that must have accompanied their view. Soldiers that had traveled from a great distance that are now sleeping on the ground had to have smelled to high heaven! Not to mention, the camels that were too numerous to count.

Our local county has an annual fair that comes to town near the end of summer. Our church put up an exhibit booth to hand out gospel tracts and paint children's faces for free. What was our location? We were within fifty feet of two camels. You guessed it, they stunk! The stench was accompanied by camel fleas that bit our ankles all week long.

Back to our story, Gideon and Purah walk into this camp filled with smelly soldiers and smelly camels. It appears that everyone's asleep, but then Gideon hears two soldiers talking. Gideon hears a man sharing a dream with one of his companions. This mans' dream speaks of a loaf of barley bread tumbling into the Midianites camp and knocking over a tent. Understand, the majority of the soldiers would have been sleeping on the ground. The general would typically sleep in a tent. This dream depicts a loaf of barley bread toppling over the Generals tent, meaning that the army would be defeated. The man's companion concludes that the dream is a real warning that Gideon and his troops are about to raid their camp. He also concludes that God was the author of the invasion. This enemy of God believed that God was going to allow Gideon to conquer the Midianites. Meanwhile, Gideon and Purah hear this conversation and their confidence in God's promise soars.

These few verses tell us a great deal about the God in which we serve. He is sovereign and providential. He is over all of creation and has a plan that no one can bring down. He has the ability to put all of the pieces of the puzzle together, mix them up, and put them back together again. In the bible we find that God throughout human history has not only prophesied extraordinary events, but He has also brought those events into reality. He is more powerful than we can imagine.

But now lets' analyze this dream a little bit. Does a loaf of barley bread really sound like Gideon? Yes. Barley is a grain that can adapt to many different climates. It would ripen quick and very easily resisted heat. Barley was also harvested before wheat and was often times fed to domestic animals. The quality of its nutrition was poor and that made it inexpensive. Because its quality was poor Barley was fed to slaves and was held in low esteem as a grain.

Do you get the picture? Gideon was the least of his tribe and his tribe was the least of the nation Israel. Gideon was an unlikely hero. The odds were stacked against him. To the world, Gideon and his band of three hundred men looked weak. They would have been considered lowly and without esteem. However, in God's eyes, Gideon and his men were the chosen vessels.

God likes using the weak things of this world to put to shame the wisdom of this world. The following passage written by the Apostle Paul applies to the life of Gideon.

1 Corinthians 1:26-31, NKJV
[26] For you see your calling, brethren, that not many wise according to the flesh, not many mighty, not many noble, are called. [27] But God has chosen the foolish things of the world to put to shame the wise, and God has chosen the weak things of the world to put to shame the things which are mighty; [28] and the base things of the world and the things which are despised God has chosen, and the things which are not, to bring to nothing the

things that are, ²⁹ *that no flesh should glory in His presence.* ³⁰ *But of Him you are in Christ Jesus, who became for us wisdom from God--and righteousness and sanctification and redemption--* ³¹ *that, as it is written, "He who glories, let him glory in the Lord."*

When the odds are stacked against God, I believe He laughs. In fact, He usually goes to great extremes to prove that He can bring the victory through anyone he desires. He does this so that He can receive the glory, so that the world will know that He exists and that He alone saves. God is always proving that He alone is our sufficiency.

In all of this, by having Gideon eavesdrop on the enemy's conversation, God is saying to Gideon, "I will keep my promise". God's resolve? The victory is yours.

It's funny how this text reveals that the enemy knew that he was a defeated foe. Our ultimate enemy is Satan and deep down he knows that he has been defeated. When you read the last book of the bible, Revelation, you find that the end of the book reveals that Jesus Christ wins. And because He wins, those in Christ, they also win. That's a promise from God, a promise that God is able to keep.

Chapter Twenty-One

"Victory God's Way"
_____

Judges 7:15-23, NKJV

15 *And so it was, when Gideon heard the telling of the dream and its interpretation, that he worshiped. He returned to the camp of Israel, and said, "Arise, for the Lord has delivered the camp of Midian into your hand."* **16** *Then he divided the three hundred men* into *three companies, and he put a trumpet into every man's hand, with empty pitchers, and torches inside the pitchers.* **17** *And he said to them, "Look at me and do likewise; watch, and when I come to the edge of the camp you shall do as I do:* **18** *When I blow the trumpet, I and all who* are *with me, then you also blow the trumpets on every side of the whole camp, and say, 'The sword of the Lord and of Gideon!' "* **19** *So Gideon and the hundred men who* were *with him came to the outpost of the camp at the beginning of the middle watch, just as they had posted the watch; and they blew the trumpets and broke the pitchers that* were *in their hands.* **20** *Then the three companies blew the trumpets and broke the pitchers--they held the torches in their left hands and the trumpets in their right hands for blowing--and they cried, "The sword of the Lord and of Gideon!"* **21** *And every man stood in his* place all around the camp; and the whole army ran and cried out and fled. ²² When the three hundred blew the trumpets, the Lord set every man's sword against his companion throughout the whole camp; and the army fled to Beth Acacia, toward Zererah, as far as the border of Abel Meholah, by Tabbath. ²³ And the men of Israel gathered together from Naphtali, Asher, and all Manasseh, and pursued the Midianites.

How do you respond when God blesses you? When God keeps His promise to you, what is your reaction? Do you jump for joy? Do you call a friend and give God the glory for all that He has done? How do you respond to God's grace?

After listening to the soldiers' interpretation of the dream, the bible says that Gideon worshipped. Not only did he worship, but he worshipped on the spot. He didn't wait until he got back to his camp. The bible says Gideon worshipped and then returned to the camp of Israel. Worshipping God is appropriate anywhere and at anytime, even while you're standing in the midst of the enemy's camp.

Worship must have a high priority in the life of a Christian. True worship takes place when we humble ourselves before our holy God and praise Him for who He is and for all that He has done. As believers we are to come together and worship corporately, but we are also encouraged to worship privately. While worshipping God we are not limited to a certain place or a certain time. Our worship of God does not hinge on our geographical location or the clock that's hanging on the wall. The Apostle Paul in Philippians 4:4 reminds us to Rejoice in the Lord always. Again I will say, rejoice!

Gideon, while standing in the enemies' camp, rejoices in the Lord. Gideon's response to God's grace was an attitude of worship.

When God blesses us and we worship Him out of love and gratitude, the next thing we should do is proclaim to others the greatness of God. Gideon returns to the camp, wakes up his army of three hundred and says, "Arise, for the Lord has delivered the camp of Midian into our hand." Gideon declares the victory. He tells his troops that God is going to keep His promise.

Let me ask you a question, have you been faithful in telling others about the greatness of God? When God blesses you and you worship Him, do you take the next step and proclaim the good news? Do you share all that God has done? Do you share with others the promises that God has made?

Gideon goes back to the camp with his increased faith and breathes even more confidence into the lives of his soldiers. Gideon talked about winning before he ever stepped foot onto the battlefield. He believed God and was willing to share his faith with his troops. Gideon's faith had now grown and his trust in God was at its greatest height. What does Gideon do? He begins to implement God's plan for the victory.

As you read Judges 7:16 you find that Gideon divides the men up into three companies and places God's weapons of warfare into their hands. The weapons Gideon gave each man were a trumpet, an empty pitcher and a lit torch. What about a sword? No. How about a shield? No. How about a helmet? No. Gideon gave each man a trumpet, a pitcher and a lit torch. I know what you're thinking, that doesn't sound like a list of weapons. I guess a person could hit someone over the head with the trumpet or the pitcher. Maybe a soldier could catch the enemy's camp on fire with the torch, but wouldn't you need more than that?

Remember the title of this section. God's way is the only way. God had instructed Gideon to hand out these items as weapons. This was God's way.

God is not limited to our definition of a weapon. When we think of a weapon, we think of guns, knives, swords and unfortunately bombs. But you know, Webster has a good definition of weapon. Webster does say that a weapon is an implement used to fight with, that sounds like our definition. However, Webster goes on to say that a weapon is anything used to get the better of an opponent. That is a broad definition. In fact, God uses that definition because in God's hands anything can become a weapon. He can get the better of an opponent using anything or anyone He chooses. For instance, you put a man like Gideon in Gods' hands', God can do whatever He decides. Let's take that a step further. Let's say God places a trumpet, a pitcher and a lit torch into the hands of three hundred men, He can still turn those objects into weapons. He, God, can get the better of any opponent with anything in His hands or with nothing in His hands. That is the power of God. Remember the weapons that we fight with don't resemble the weapons of this world. The Apostle Paul reminds us in 1 Corinthians 10:4 *"For the weapons of our warfare are not carnal but mighty in God for pulling down strongholds".*

In our text, Gideon has placed these unlikely objects into the hands of his troops. These ordinary objects have become the weapons of God. How is God going to use these three hundred men with these unlikely weapons?

Remember, the troops had been divided up into three companies. These companies were to surround the enemies' camp and were to keep their eyes on Gideon. Gideon in verse seventeen says, "Look at me and do likewise; watch, and when I come to the edge of the camp you shall do as I do". We have to pause and not miss this teachable moment in scripture. In a sense Gideon says, "Do whatever I do", in other words, "follow my lead". As you have read this book you can't help but notice that God has been transforming young Gideon into a great leader. As a leader, you cannot expect people to follow you if you are unwilling to do the very thing that you are calling your followers to do. Modeling God's vision for those you lead is crucial. It's a must. It's not optional. If a leader models an action successfully then he/she can lead others to follow their example. That is exactly what Gideon is doing in verse seventeen. He says, "watch me and do likewise". With that said, what did Gideon model for these troops? What was God's strategy for the victory?

The three companies were to surround the camp in the middle of the night. They were to conceal their lit torch within the empty pitcher. At Gideon's signal they were to break the pitcher, hold the torch in their left hand while holding the trumpet with their right hand. Then they were to blow the trumpet and cry out, "the sword of the Lord and of Gideon!" How about that plan? Who else would dream up a strategy like that, except God? Only God could bring the victory this way. And that's exactly what He did.

We find in verse twenty one that the three hundred men surrounded the enemy's camp. The bible says that "every man stood in his place all around the camp". Then simultaneously, all three hundred men blew their trumpets and cried out, "the sword of the Lord and of Gideon". What else did they do? The soldiers witnessed God fight the battle His way. The bible says in verse twenty two that "the Lord set every man's sword against his companion and caused the enemy to flee." After hearing three hundred trumpets blow in unison, after hearing three hundred men cry out, the Lord confuses the Midianite army and they begin to kill one another and disperse. What did Gideon's army of three hundred do? They call together the rest of the men within the tribes and they pursued the Midianites as they fled. They plundered the enemies belongings, they seize the watering places as far as Beth Barah and the Jordan, and they capture two princes and beheaded them (see Judges 7:24-25).

How did God bring the victory? What did God consider His way of winning this battle?

The following is a list of great truths that we can conclude from the victory that was accomplished God's way:
1) God is able to win any battle with or without our participation. However, he often times chooses to include us in accomplishing His perfect will.
2) God often times uses unlikely heroes in the process. In our text God calls a weak man named Gideon and transforms him into a leader that would obey the Lords commands.
3) This same man after being tested by God steps up to the plate and goes to bat for the Lord's vision for victory. He steps out by faith and compels others to follow the Lord.
4) Gideon compels others to be faithful, while he himself models faithfulness.

The following are some spiritual nuggets that flow from this victory that was accomplished God's way.

The weapons that Gideon's men used are similar to the weapons we use as we battle for souls.

Trumpet – Gideon's men were to carry a trumpet in their hands and were to blow the trumpet at a given time. Trumpets in the bible were used for different purposes. The Priests would blow the trumpet during services of sacrifice, especially to signal the Day of Atonement. Another type of trumpet called a shophar was used as a signaling instrument. It was used to assemble an army, to sound an attack and to sound an alarm.

Today, we battle for souls with a trumpet in our hand, the gospel. We, as believers, are called to sound an alarm to a lost and dieing world. The church is to assemble around this instrument of righteousness, the gospel, the blood of the Lord Jesus Christ. This trumpet, the gospel, also sounds an attack to our enemy Satan and reminds him that the Lord is mighty to save.

Today, God wants to bring victory over sin, death and the grave to people everywhere. We help accomplish this great task by blowing the trumpet, by preaching the gospel. For people to have this type of victory the gospel must be preached. It is the greatest weapon in this battle for souls.

^{13} *For* "whoever calls on the name of the Lord shall be saved." ^{14} *How then shall they call on Him in whom they have not believed? And how shall they believe in Him of whom they have not heard? And how shall they hear without a preacher?* ^{15} *And how shall they preach unless they are sent? As it is written:* "How beautiful are the feet of those who preach the gospel of peace, Who bring glad tidings of good things!" ^{16} *But they have not all obeyed the gospel. For Isaiah says,* "Lord, who has believed our report?" ^{17} *So then faith* comes *by hearing, and hearing by the word of God.* **Romans 10:13-17 (NKJV)**

<u>An Empty Pitcher</u> – Gideon's men were to also carry an empty pitcher. In biblical times, pitchers came in all kinds of shapes and sizes. And although they may look different from one another, each pitcher shares a common purpose. That purpose is to carry something that's needed.

Today, we are those empty pitchers, earthen vessels if you will. We, as human beings, come in all kinds of shapes and sizes. And although we look different from one another, we also, like different pitchers, share a common purpose. That purpose is for us to carry something that is needed, something valuable.

In fact, we were each born to carry someone else deep within us. That someone is Jesus Christ.

But notice, Gideon's men were to bring along an empty pitcher. Before a person can accept Jesus Christ into their heart as their personal savior, they must empty themselves of self. A person must come to the conclusion that they are nothing without Christ and that their sin can only be forgiven by God through the blood of Christ. A person that is willing to empty themselves for the glory of God is a great weapon in the hand of God. But now as we look to Gideon's men these pitchers didn't stay empty for long, did they?

A Lit Torch – The next weapon that Gideon placed into his men's hands was a lit torch. This torch was to be placed within the empty pitcher and at a certain time the soldiers were to break their pitchers and allow only the torch to be seen. In fact, as this winning strategy unfolded, the uncircumcised enemies of God could only see the light of the torch. The empty pitcher could not be seen, only the light.

When a person accepts Jesus Christ into their life and abandons self, the light of Christ comes to dwell within that person's heart. As God's redemptive strategy for the world unfolds, God's will for the believers, "His army", is for our earthen vessel, "our lives", to not be seen by this lost world. When we walk by faith and allow God to bring victories in our own lives His way, the lost and dieing world will only see His light within us. We, the pitcher, the earthen vessel, are broken and are on the ground.

The End Result – The world hears a trumpet, the gospel, being sounded by a flaming torch that is burning brightly.

The lost don't see religion they see the light of Christ.

The lost don't see you and I, earthen vessels, they see the light of Christ.

When the gospel is sounded in unity, the lost don't hear denominations, they hear Christ.

And if they will listen and believe, God will bring them victory over sin, death and the grave, His way. And by the way, salvation only occurs God's way, not ours.

In our text, God brought the victory His way. He used an unlikely hero in Gideon and He used unusual objects and turned them into weapons. The bottom line is this, God kept His promise to Gideon and to the nation Israel. His goal was to draw His people back to Himself. His delight was to provide a much needed savior, and He did.

Did you find yourself in this story? Did you discover the fact that God can use anyone at anytime for His glory? Did you figure out that God not only wants to use you but can use you? Did you hear his call to redemption? Did you hear and feel the heartbeat of God? Did you hear God's heart beating for souls?

Today, <u>you can</u> live the victorious Christian life. <u>You can</u> serve the God of this universe and bring glory and honor to His name. <u>You can</u> lead others to follow God's plan. After reading about the life of Gideon, can you now begin to see <u>The Gideon In You</u> ? Can you see the leader within you? Can you see the Spirit of God working within your life? If so, will you follow the example of Gideon and blow the trumpet, the gospel? Will you allow the light of Christ to outshine your earthen vessel? I hope so, because a lost and dieing world is counting on seeing <u>The Gideon In You.</u>

Let your light so shine before men, that they may see your good works and glorify your Father in heaven. Matthew 5:16 (NKJV)

www.ingramcontent.com/pod-product-compliance
Lightning Source LLC
Chambersburg PA
CBHW061444040426
42450CB00007B/1198